Minnie Mary Lee

Basil, Beatrice, Ethel, or, Three-times-three

An interesting story of real life

Minnie Mary Lee

Basil, Beatrice, Ethel, or, Three-times-three
An interesting story of real life

ISBN/EAN: 9783741133664

Manufactured in Europe, USA, Canada, Australia, Japa

Cover: Foto ©Andreas Hilbeck / pixelio.de

Manufactured and distributed by brebook publishing software (www.brebook.com)

Minnie Mary Lee

Basil, Beatrice, Ethel, or, Three-times-three

Basil, Beatrice; Ethel;

— OR, —

Three-Times-Three.

— AN —

INTERESTING STORY OF REAL LIFE.

*In memoria æterna erit justus;
Desiderium peccatorum peribit.*
—Psalm cxi.

By MRS. JULIA A. A. WOOD,
(MINNIE MARY LEE.)

BALTIMORE:
PUBLISHED BY JOHN B. PIET & CO.
174 W. Baltimore Street.
1883.

CONTENTS.

	PAGE.
CHAPTER I.	
A MYSTERIOUS DEATH..	1
CHAPTER II.	
THE NORTHWARD FLITTING...............................	6
CHAPTER III.	
ETHEL'S WELCOME...	9
CHAPTER IV.	
LOIS WALSINGHAM'S CHOICE.............................	13
CHAPTER V.	
A COLD COLLATION..	19
CHAPTER VI.	
"THE GLORIOUS FOURTH" AT SUNAPEE.............	23
CHAPTER VII.	
BASIL BRAUN VISITS "BIRD'SNEST"...................	32
CHAPTER VIII.	
THE NAME OF BASIL BRAUN................................	38
CHAPTER IX.	
THE FOUR FRIENDS...	46
CHAPTER X.	
EXCITING SCENE AT RED ROCK.........................	55
CHAPTER XI.	
DINNER AT THE PARSONAGE.............................	64
CHAPTER XII.	
AFTER THE GREAT DAY.....................................	70
CHAPTER XIII.	
ETHEL'S OPINION OF BOOK-WORMS...................	76

CONTENTS.

CHAPTER XIV.
Learning Something New 85

CHAPTER XV.
"A Dastardly Outrage" 100

CHAPTER XVI.
Father English at "Bird'snest" 111

CHAPTER XVII.
The Court of Justice—Mrs. Huldah at the Key-Hole 122

CHAPTER XVIII.
From St. Mark's—Whither? 135

CHAPTER XIX.
Mr. Ferrol's Bishop—Christmas at Claremont 148

CHAPTER XX.
Mr. Ferrol's Successor—An Inheritance 157

CHAPTER XXI.
A Stranger at "Bird'snest" and a Reunion 167

CHAPTER XXII.
A New Project—Considerable Consultation 179

CHAPTER XXIII.
Fair "Bird'snest" by the Lake—Hatred and Revenge 187

CHAPTER XXIV.
At Last—Disenthralled 198

CHAPTER XXV.
Sunapee Talks of the Marriage while our Friends Journey Southward 211

CHAPTER XXVI.
Youthful Lovers—Crosses and Crowns 218

CHAPTER XXVII.
Confession of Octave Geoffrion—Marriage Bells—White Veil 233

BASIL, BEATRICE AND ETHEL;

— OR, —

THREE-TIMES-THREE.

CHAPTER I.

A MYSTERIOUS DEATH.

ALL astir with excitement was the city of Santa Fé. On a litter, borne by four burros, had been brought in from the mountains the mutilated remains of Colonel Willoughby, for years a prominent resident of this metropolis of New Mexico.

He had been a man of great energy and will; he had a cool head, a warm heart, and a genial nature. An American by birth, he had married an intelligent Spanish senora, whose father had been a man of wealth and influence. By this wife he had two children, a son and a daughter, lovely in disposition and beautiful in person.

The house of Colonel Willoughby was in the suburbs of the city. An adobe house of one story, built in a square, with a plazeta, or small courtyard, in the centre. Luxuriant gardens and delicious orchards and vineyards environed this fair and pleasant dwelling.

A month—one little month ago the proud, happy master of this princely Mexican home had sat upon his richly caparisoned horse by his own gates.

Carlotta, his beloved wife, shading with fair hand her liquid Andalusian eyes, looked out of them, half smiling, half weeping, her last fond *adios*. Francisco and Beatrice, children of sixteen and twelve, stood one on either side of the handsome father, patting the mane of the princely steed, or smoothing and caressing the gold and velvet trappings of his caparison.

When the mother had spoken her last words in her own musical tongue, the children said theirs in pure English, blending fond good-byes with urgent entreaties for as speedy a return as possible.

It appeared as if all would delay the inevitable parting; but last moments must come—and the three by the gates stood weeping, watching until the Colonel was out of sight. A score or more of Mexicans had accompanied Colonel Willoughby, all mounted, and full of delight that they were permitted to share such noble company.

Did the three—the lonely Spanish wife, the loving son and daughter—have premonition of what one little month should bring?

Yes, all Santa Fé was astir, for Colonel Willoughby had been brought in mangled and dead; his faithful Mexicans, each leading his mule or his burro, following the stately tread of the noble horse which seemed to know his master was no' more and that he was being borne before him!

How had it happened? was the breathless, multiplied question. A summing up of the statements and cross-questionings was this:

Colonel Willoughby, with his companions, had encamped for the night. They had been visited by two strangers, who spoke only in English, and to Colonel Willoughby alone. In compliance with their apparent solicitations he went with them from camp. Miguel Lucéro, a favorite and attendant of the Colonel, attempted to follow, but was waived back. Soon was heard from a promontory above, and at right of them, the sound of voices and of blows. Looking upward, they beheld their leader contending with the two upon the very verge of the precipice.

Miguel and several others rushed to the terrible scene of conflict. Those who remained, spell-bound, watched the issue, which soon came. Two figures went over the precipice together; the third lay weltering upon the ground. Rapiers and knives had been freely used. It needed but a thrust from Miguel's stiletto "To open Hades," as he expressed it, to the soul of this stranger, whom, in their blind fury, they pushed also over the precipice.

No life was in either of the bodies that had first gone down. They were terribly cut by the deadly knives, and the fall—well, it was thus Colonel Willoughby had met this shocking, this untimely death.

But who had been these enemies of the murdered man? Had Colonel Willoughby an enemy in the world? Had he not been a resident of Santa Fé for more than a score of years, honored, trusted and beloved? But what was this mission on which Colonel Willoughby had gone out? No one knew. His attendants stated that he had visited several mines, making particular observations and surveys, and he was on the eve of a special journey, having made ten days' provision for the same, and this was the end of all!

Had the Mexicans examined the clothes or the weapons of these malicious marauders? Miguel had simply possessed himself of one weapon, that which he drew from near the heart of the man on the cliff, but this was the gem-handled stiletto of Colonel Willoughby! And all was peace at the sunny home in the suburbs of Santa Fé. Who should have the heart to disturb it? Who could do it better than Father Fielon, who was the friend and spiritual adviser of the family? Accordingly, he went thither, growing more and more sad as he neared the premises, yet striving to nerve himself for the dreaded task.

The body had been taken to the undertakers, and, by aid of the good Sisters, made comely as possible for the last agonized look of the bereaved family.

And still speculations were rife as to the true reason of the Colonel's death. Had he not been foully dealt with by his comrades? True, he had been beloved by them all; but, in the heat of passion, had they not become angered against him?

A delegation was organized, Miguel at the head, (unknown to his companions), for a reconnoisance of the alleged scene of the murder.

Meanwhile the dead was honored by the most imposing funeral. The great Cathedral was filled almost to suffocation by throngs of kneeling suppliants, who bowed themselves low in tearful prayers for repose of the soul of him who had met a "sudden and unprovided death."

Music, solemn and sweet, flowed forth in psalm and chant. Incense sweetened the air, already thick with prayers and sighs. Sobs and wails of widow and children were blended with wail and sob of the multitude, which was stirred as with one impulse of grief and sympathy.

O sad and solemn mystery of Life and Death, why long we so to tear the veil, when so soon it shall be revealed to every human soul!

CHAPTER II.

THE NORTHWARD FLITTING.

MOUNT SUNAPEE, N. H., May 13, 18—

MY DEAR COUSINS—I add a word, to go with mamma's, to tell you how delighted we are that you are coming. All the Mount rejoices, and is glad in so unusual an anticipation as that of receiving visitors from that old historic town, which I used to study about in geography, and dreamed of as being more distant than the stars. Little did I then think I had an uncle living there, whose wife and little ones were natives of that far-off City of the Holy Faith!

And now, how very wonderful, that poor uncle should so mysteriously have been murdered, and so much of his property been unlawfully taken from you! Mamma and I cannot comprehend it. But you are so welcome to our own home. We have a perfect bird's-nest of a home, it is so cosy and nice—that is, in summer. It is only just spring now, and by time you arrive it will be glorious June; flowers will be in bloom, birds will sing, and you will see for yourself how beautiful are sky, earth and water; for, indeed, we live near the shore of Lake Sunapee—a sheet of clearest water—on which we will enjoy many boat-rides. I am so thankful one of you is a boy, for he can take care of us. I never had a brother, nor ever saw a boy-cousin. How can I wait till you come!

Do you not think a story ever so much nicer, where there is a fine boy, and he the elder? I do; and my life, which has been so tame, spent alone with mamma, is about to have a new leaf, and be just like a story. I am sure you will be ample protection, dear cousin Francisco, through all those mountain passes, of your mother and sister; you will have a revolver for every bandit. How I long to see you with my own eyes, and listen to your wonderful tales. What a full sheet! Mamma, as she tells you herself, is well, and I am also; and so are the birds and the cats; that is all of us.

Your affectionate cousin,
ETHEL FORSYTH.

Three years had passed since their great affliction, and the Willoughby family now found themselves, through a series of inexplicable circumstances, greatly reduced in property. It appeared as if the one enemy of the late Colonel still existed, and was determined to ruin all who bore his name; although there was no ostensible enemy, unless, indeed, the cousin of Carlotta might be deemed such. But he professed for her great kindness. His proffers of friendship were constant, and his expressions of sympathy always fervent and tender. But Carlotta viewed him with distrust and disfavor, as always she had done. Her own father had some years previously met with a violent death, and this nephew of his had produced papers making himself principal heir, to the exclusion of the only child, Carlotta.

However, no one disputed Octave Geoffrion's claim He had been his uncle's favorite, and it had been well known that the uncle never favored the union of his child with the man she married. But Colonel Willoughby, proud and independent, had all the treasure he wanted in his beautiful Carlotta, and, with his own strong hand and fertile brain, had carved out a fortune and an honorable name.

Suffice to say, after three years of litigation the widow found herself with little, save the lonely homestead whereat she had dwelt and a few thousand in ready money.

Correspondence had been kept up with Colonel Willonghby's only sister in the far North.

Weary with cares and vexations, Carlotta at length yielded to her sister-in-law's kind invitations to visit her. Her children's importunities had largely contributed to induce her to this resolution. A brisk correspondence had been kept up by the lively cousins. Ethel was a year older than Beatrice—and in one sense was so old, and in another so young (judged by her letters), as to be an enigma to the youthful Southerners.

Another reason, and perhaps the only one which would have found favor with Father Fielon for her undertaking this long and perilous journey, was the state of Carlotta's health. She could not recover from the shock of her grief. To her the light had gone out from all the world. New scenes might arouse her to a fresh interest in life.

It had not been publicly known that Mrs. Willoughby was to take so long a journey, or expected to be so long absent. She was to visit a friend, who was now Lady Superior in a convent in Colorado; thus much only was known. The beautiful Willoughby place was rented for a couple of years—and the widow and children commenced their long and wearisome journey to the white hills of the granite State.

Had they foreseen how long and fatiguing, they might have set forth with less buoyant spirits. They were in company of several Jesuit Fathers and two or three lay gentlemen who had come out health-seekers, and who, restored and comforted, were about to return joyfully to home and friends.

CHAPTER III.

ETHEL'S WELCOME.

TWO new rooms had been added to "Bird's-nest" cottage. These had been fitted up with all the elegancies accessible. It had been Ethel's peculiar province to beautify the one devoted to her hero, Francisco. She would have quite despoiled every other part of the house to do honor to this one apartment, had not her more prudent mother put forth a staying hand. She would remark more than once:

"Remember, my child, your boy-cousin is not the only guest we shall have to entertain. You must not monopolize Francisco, but include his sister as well, in all your affectionate preparations."

"Of course, mamma, I shall do that. But we girls can take care of ourselves. Beatrice and I shall both wait on Francisco. He is her brother and my cousin. But I shall claim the greater part of him while he stays with us. Hasn't Beatrice had him all her life? Pity if she can't give him up to me for a *little* while. Bless her! I shall take him anyhow—stilettos, revolvers and all."

"But, Ethel, do you know he is three years older than yourself—a youth of nineteen, perhaps tall of his age?"

"Isn't that all the better? I am fifteen and almost a half (I will have that half included), and soon I shall be a young lady. If I were sixteen now, sweet sixteen! I do hope Francisco is fine looking! What if, after all, he should be a fright, or even only as ordinary as Basil Braun! How stupid that would be! But if he is real handsome, he shall go with me to meeting, and he shall astonish all Sunapee by riding on my own pony faster than ever I dared to ride. And if he prove grand and nice, as I so hope he will be, and am so *awfully* afraid he won't be, I will—well—what won't I do—I'll be tempted to carry him around for a show. If he only would be like a hero in a book!"

And thus Ethel's fertile fancy dwelt on the possibilities, while her busy hand made knick-knacks, embroidered a footstool, made pillow-shams, and did many, many things too numerous to particularize.

The Willoughbys arrived not quite so soon as expected. More time had been consumed in the journey than had been anticipated, and Ethel's patience had become very much tried.

Day after day had she arranged her golden curls in their prettiest, and in their pink fillet of satin set her daintiest rose, and, in snowiest ruffled apron of white, stood upon the broad granite door-steps, on the only particular corner of which she might catch a glimmer of the coach through the trees. And after each disappointment she watched the concord coach go on its way, tears of vexation dimming her blue eyes, and her fair fingers tearing in pieces the pretty bouquet designed for an offering of welcome.

At length said Ethel to her mother:

"They will not come while I watch for them so eagerly. Rachel told me so, and said while she was in a hurry, waiting for the pot to boil, it would never bubble. But if she turned to do something else, and forget the pot, directly she would hear the puff—puffing. So, at four o'clock, I shall not take my stand on the doorstep, but shall take my dish of meal and feed my dear little chicks."

And this did Ethel. And while, intent on this piece of daily duty, the homeliest and tiniest of the brood held tightly in her hands and snuggled up under her chin, an apparition stood suddenly before her.

And such an apparition! The frail feathered atom of chickendom was instantly dropped, and both hands clasped the hand of the tallest, handsomest youth the world had ever seen! This was Ethel's instant verdict. What a figure! Only the fabled Apollo's could equal it. What dark, dreaming eyes, full of mirth and brightness, like those described in the sweetest of her novels. Such a rich, charming complexion, without a tinge of color—all the color the red lips held, from which came the most melodious voice that had ever fallen upon her ear. More grand and beautiful than she had dreamed, was her cousin Francisco!

And stoutly Ethel averred, when in presence of mother and kindred, that, had she waited for them and watched, they would not have come; no, never!

Equally, almost, was Ethel charmed by the mother and sister of Francisco; for it was through him they so delighted her. As her aunt and cousins, they were to be honored and beloved; as nearest and dearest to Francisco, they were to be adored.

The aunt, Carlotta, was slightly above medium size—a pretty, interesting specimen of the pure Spanish type. Her gentle manners, somewhat languid, were most pleasing. Her gracious smile was full of sweetness and benignity. Her imperfect English, instead of a detraction, was a charm. There was all about her that simplicity, blended with gentle dignity, which proclaimed her a lady and rendered her most winning.

Her children closely resembled herself: Beatrice the least, however. In the dark hair of the latter was a shade of brown, and the eye, though liquid and beaming, had not that intense depth of blackness which was seen in mother and brother. The complexion, too, of Beatrice had a hue of rosiness, which the others perfectly lacked.

Ethel's delight knew no bounds. Her quick perceptions took in at once that this instant admiration was mutual. Yes, they admired this fair rose of the Northern clime, such a contrast to themselves, and took her to their hearts at once. And Ethel kept thinking how proud she should be of her relatives, these strangers from so far! Had Sunapee Mount ever seen a Spanish cavalier—they should behold him; or Spanish senora, or senorina—here were they for its admiration.

CHAPTER IV.

LOIS WALSINGHAM'S CHOICE.

MRS. FORSYTH, a delicate little lady, below medium height, had scarcely reached her thirty-fifth year. She, too, had been a widow since the babyhood of her only child. Lois Forsyth's father had been for many years a sea-captain, sailing from Gloucester as regularly as the seasons came around. Late in life he married a youthful widow, Mrs. Willoughby, much his junior in years, to whom he became devotedly attached. After taking her with him on several voyages, finding she wearied of sea-life, and unwilling to sail without her, the Captain sold out and withdrew altogether from sea-faring.

With a handsome competence, he retired unto this romantic wild of New Hampshire, selected the finest portion on the shores of Lake Sunapee, erected a germ of a cottage, which he adorned with many curious trophies from far lands and seas, and here, with his love, contemplated spending "the remnant of that day that must be mortal to them both."

After two years' residence at "Bird'snest," (the Captain had chosen a cozy name for his home, you may believe,) and five years of married life, two great and unexpected events occurred in the household: the birth of a daughter, and the death of the wife—only a few weeks intervening.

Though the ex-Captain pined and grieved, even tore his hair and wept, he was strong and mighty in health and vigor, and did not die, as he had prayed, but lived on for twenty years, not ceasing to remember the lost love, but receiving consolation from the costly price of her precious life—his daughter, Lois.

For Captain Walsingham would have the child christened Lois. Lois had been the mother's name and the grandmother's from generations untraceable, and the name must not die out from fault of his.

And this name, of olden fashion, was to him the sweetest of all womanly names. Why? Because associated with all womanly virtues in the person of his wife.

Woman, wife and mother! Why see ye not to it, that, through all the succeeding years, ye keep holy the vow made before the altar to love and honor him to whom you have pledged your life and your all? *Command* your husband's love by a constant deference and affectionate attention. *Deserve* his homage, nay, his reverence, by your truthfulness, integrity, devotion to his interests, and by loving kindness and sweet charity to all. *Win* his kindness and confidence by being ever kind and truthful. So, shall you enshrine yourself in his heart of hearts, and sanctify the beautiful sacrament of marriage.

How do this, is it questioned? How subdue the temper? how conquer a rebellious spirit? how return injury, insult, galling words, by gentle silence, quiet words and sweet patience? By cherishing and cultivating the spirit which the Christ-Child, ever-living, teaches—the spirit of forgiveness, submission, charity.

Captain Walsingham revered woman. So would all men hold her in highest esteem, did she herself, as wife and mother, carry herself piously and womanly.

The faithful master of "Bird'snest" took no second mate. Sibyl Lester, a cousin of his own, assumed care of his house, while a nurse, and afterward a governess, kept constant vigilance over the child.

We have stated that Captain Walsingham married a widow. This lady had one son, George Willoughby, who had remained at school during the whole period of his mother's second marriage. As she died, he never even visited her at the home in Sunapee, but, having finished his studies, he wandered South, and, therefore, had known his step-father and half-sister only by epistolary correspondence.

This, with the latter, had been kept up until his death.

Lois grew in health and prettiness. She had not remarkable beauty of face, but great sweetness of expression, blended with that of much decisiveness of character. In this she inherited her father's firmness of will, with her mother's gentle nobility, dignity and grace.

Needless to say, that, growing to maidenhood, she became, as it were, queen of Sunapee Mount. Rustic farmers looked at her askance. Rural maidens shyly nodded the head, admiring, yet vaguely wondering whence the difference betwixt her and them. Fathers and mothers lay the superiority, which they saw and felt without comprehending, to an abundance of this world's goods, and to Captain Walsingham having seen so much of the world!

Lois was taught languages, music and painting at

home, because her father could not bear her out of his sight for one whole day together.

Painting was the young lady's preference; and while, having become eighteen, she was no longer under rule of a governess, she still pursued this favorite study, or pastime as it was with her.

She had a fine knowledge of perspective, and had taken in and put upon canvas the finest views of all the surrounding country.

Captain Walsingham was an old man now, and yearly growing more and more feeble. What would become of his daughter when he should be no longer on earth? This question was becoming painful. She had had suitors, but none of them pleased her. None of them had pleased the Captain either, with one exception. This was the youthful rector of St. Mark's Episcopal Church of the adjoining town of Duxbury. Rev. Mr. James Ferrol had lately succeeded the former incumbent, deceased. The Captain and his daughter had been noticed among his congregation. They were not members of, but attendants at, St. Mark's, and the young clergyman deeming that they ought to be members, and thinking it a great fault on somebody that they were not so, made it in his way to call over to "Bird's-nest."

With the old gentleman he was pleased; with the young lady delighted. He went away from this pleasantest shore of Lake Sunapee firmly resolved to bring both father and daughter into St. Mark's fold, and fully convinced it would be an easy matter to induce Miss Lois to become Mrs. James Ferrol whenever he might say the word. And he went to work accordingly.

The result is soon told. His religious arguments

were listened to politely, but appeared to have made slight impression, since no action ensued towards joining the holy communion of St. Mark's.

His speedy wooing met with a courteous but decided refusal; and James Ferrol returned to his lonely parish home, and straightway viewed himself in his whole-length mirror, trying to discover what could be amiss in him that the offer of his hand and heart should be thus hotly refused. He turned himself around and around; surveyed his wavy hair, his intellectual brow, fine eyes and white neck-tie—in fine, surveyed himself from top to toe, considered his elegant bearing, his ministerial air, and was non-plussed; he could not make it out. Had he been at all deep or penetrating, he would have read one word through and over all that *tout ensemble* of his make-up, and that one word would have enlightened his *conceit*.

Rev. James Ferrol made a resolve: he would return to New York, and bring back as bride one of the twenty young ladies who were all ready to fall at his feet, thereby showing to the old hulk of a sea-captain, and to the proud minx, his daughter, that there were as good fish in the sea, etc. He went: and much of the conceit was taken out of him, when he found it was not until he knelt to the thirteenth that he was listened to with favor. And even this thirteenth he was not prepared to take; for when he could have her, she had lost her charms. He wondered he had not discovered sooner how old she looked, how sharp she was, how loud her voice, and how ungentle her movements! Duxbury would be astonished at his taste! Lois Walsingham would laugh at his choice of an old maid!

No, it would never do. Besides, something *might*

happen; in course of events Lois might become fatherless, and she might recall her decision. At all events, he returned b.ideless to Duxbury, a trifle less conscious and pompous.

In this case, had Lois said yes, the father would not have said nay, but, as it was, he would not venture one word to influence her decision.

But he was becoming anxious.

One day a stranger appeared at the cottage bearing letters of introduction to Captain Walsingham.

This was Paul Forsyth, a handsome young artist, whose pencil was his passion. He was the son of an old friend of the Captain, and was therefore received most cordially.

And Lois too was a painter!

And what should happen, but that these two lovers of nature and art should love each other; which they did, with cordial consent of the father; and Rev. James Ferrol had the pleasure or pain of performing the marriage ceremony.

CHAPTER V.

A COLD COLLATION.

PAUL FORSYTH and Lois, his wife, had been a very happy couple. Captain Walsingham died in his seventieth year, blessing them and the infant daughter which had been born to them. Less than one year afterward Paul was thrown from a carriage, receiving mortal injury. The spinal cord was affected: for three months he lay upon a bed of pain and wasting, when death, angel of peace to him, but of woe to his wife, mercifully bore him to rest.

From henceforth, Lois Forsyth lived a lonely, quiet life. She lay away, out of sight forever, the pencils, palettes and easels that had been his or her own. Never again touched the pencil. For her, all nature had undergone a change, and she lived in a darkened world, whose light was her baby girl. This child Paul had named Etheldred for his own mother; and after he had gone (yes, gone for a while) Lois called her Ethel Paul, thinking to call her by both names, an idea she soon abandoned, so painful was the dear name to recall.

So Lois and little Ethel, with Sibyl and Rachel, who promised servitude for life, lived at "Bird'snest," quietly, for many years. The course pursued by Captain Walsingham with Lois, she, in her turn, had followed with Ethel. For the most part she had kept a governess, though giving much of her own time to the training of her daughter.

But now, since the Spanish innovation was to take place, Ethel was to have one long, happy holiday. The governess was to go into other pastures, green or barren.

Three hours a day practice was to be three hours or more, just as was Ethel's own sweet will. Infinitesimals, fluxions, spheroids—all these things should haunt her no more. For a while, at least, she was not to be distracted with those dreadful Punic wars, and have her heart lacerated by the tragic lives of English queens and French kings, and awful tales of religious persecution. Ah, would it not be glorious! No book but the grand book of Nature spread out so lovely before her! Body and soul grew expansive at the thought.

In this state of reaction and perfect freedom had Ethel met her Spanish cousins. Even Mrs. Forsyth was surprised and charmed at this sudden rebounding of her child. Never had she seen in her such force and enthusiasm of character. No more could she think her dull or uninteresting.

June had already lapsed into July when the travelers arrived. The "glorious Fourth" was to be celebrated at Sunapee Mount, on the large square known as the Muster-Field.

This celebration had taken place annually, from all time within memory of oldest inhabitant; but it happened this particular year there were to be unusual demonstrations and observances.

Until one year previous, Sunapee Mount, as occasion

required, had provided herself with a lawyer from Duxbury; but now a Mr. Albert Billings from abroad—that is from some other country—who had first visited Sunapee Mount village as a pedagogue, then as a suitor and accepted lover of Miss Lemantha Reubens, the Baptist minister's daughter, had established an office in a store on one of the "Four Corners," and announced himself an attorney-at-law.

Sunapee Mount had at length a leader. In nothing could the rising young man show more his skill and efficiency than in inaugurating a new programme for Fourth of July.

With dignity he arose from his pew in the Baptist church the Sunday preceding the patriotic commemoration. His father-in-law, the Rev. preacher, had just pronounced the Benediction. Mrs. Lemantha, blushing as pink as her still fresh bridal artificials, looked steadily at her feathered fan, the first ever seen in that region, while her admired lord read a synopsis of what might be expected upon the coming and glorious occasion.

First, all should gather at the church. All should be arrayed neatly in their best. All, or as many as could do so, should rob their gardens and bring treasures of flowers.

A procession should be formed, marching by twos, until the indicated grove should be reached, wherein tables would be laid, from which each and all would partake of "a cold collation."

Here Mr. Billings stopped to breathe, that all might ponder upon the unusual and great word he had used. This great word *was* revolved in each mind. What *did* it mean? A cold collation! What could be cold on a

Fourth of July? No solution could have been given, even had the lawyer waited; but he went on:

"After this cold collation (pause) the children, if they wish, can proceed to sport upon the old, time-honored muster field, while near the grove the 'Declaration of Independence' will be read by—by Esquire Billings! and Mrs. Lemantha Billings will read an original Ode to the day; and her father, Rev. Joshua Reubens, will give an oration on the heroes of the Revolution, and Dr. Buncombe will make a speech on the same immortal subject. The choir, headed by Joshua Reubens, Jr., will sing 'Old Hundred;' then Mrs. Dr. Buncombe will call up her Sunday school, which will sing sacred songs and recite several stirring odes and hymns, among which will be the 'Star-Spangled Banner,' etc., etc., after which"—but we will follow Esquire Billings no farther.

The great day came, and the younger portion of "Bird'snest's" happy family sallied forth. Apparently they had heeded the injunction to be well dressed, and to carry flowers, for in both respects they were *au fait*, though this must have been by coincidence, as they had not been present to hear the lawyer's dictation.

Ethel's pony and phaeton were made to carry three for once, and merrily the trio laughed as they went up hill and down, till at length they arrived at the grove.

For, Ethel had voted that it would be most stupid to go to the meeting-house, and walk down in heat and dust with a procession of gay country folk; therefore they would drive about and see the "town," until exercises should be well under way.

Thus it happened, being in no haste, that they did not arrive until the Declaration was receiving a great deal of strength and eloquence from Esquire Billings' stentorian lungs.

CHAPTER VI.

"THE GLORIOUS FOURTH" AT SUNAPEE.

THAT production so wonderful to the youthful intellect which has known only rural existence, viz., "The Fourth of July Oration," was delivered by Rev. Mr. Reubens in a squeaky voice, pitched high as possible, and with many and violent gesticulations, judging from which the unsophisticated Sunapeeians pronounced the whole thing a masterpiece, and Mr. Reubens a prince of orators.

While the multitude was still marveling and admiring, and Mr. Reubens still wiping with his red silken bandana the profuse perspiration from his glowing face, Mr. Billings hastened to announce: "Mrs. Lemantha Billings will now read an *'Original Ode'* suitable for the occasion," proceeding to give place to the blushing young matron, who mounted the rostrum (an overturned dry-goods box), and tremblingly unrolled her scroll.

Intense silence prevailed. Every mother's baby had been coaxed or cuffed to stillness. Every urchin from the muster-field had bade good-bye to sport, and stood spell-bound at that new and unheard-of spectacle—a woman reading in public.

How flattering was this hush of expectation!

Yet, what a disappointment, particularly to the boys, who could see only and could not hear; for Mrs. Lemantha's voice was weak and sing-y; and though she had gone through a course of training by her ambitious husband, who wished it to be understood that he had married a woman of talent, she gave very little credit to him, to herself, or to woman at large.

Her "Ode" consisted of sixty-one verses. And though little was heard, save by those within the first circle of hearers, the spell of a "woman speaker" held all silent and subdued to the close.

We will subjoin the first verses as a specimen of the whole:

> "O Fourth July—great day thou art
>   And strong thou dost appeal
> Unto each patriotic heart
>   That has the sense to feel.
> We who stand upon this ground,
>   Ready to feast on pies and buns,
> Can little know the fright they felt
>   Who faced the deadly guns.
>
> And we should honor all the men
>   Who fought for us and bled,
> For, if we too had been there then,
>   We too should have been dead—
> That is, if we hadn't run and fled,
>   As many of us would,
> And then we shouldn't been to-day
>   Enrolled among the good.
>
> O, it must be an awful thing
>   To face the cannon's roar,
> And see the men and horses fall
>   A weltering in their gore.

And to be shot like yelping dogs,
And stabbed till they are slain;
And roll about like floating logs,
All in most horrid pain, etc., etc.

This effusion was finished, and Mrs. Lemantha gracefully withdrew—that is, gracefully as she could do under the circumstances, considering she stepped from the rostrum upon the couchant form of a dog, which turned "like a floating log," though not so silently, and the distinguished oratress of the day would have fallen and been bitten had she not been immediately rescued, and the canine intruder (which, perhaps, had meant to show his appreciation) been batoned furiously away by the master of ceremonies.

Great applause rent the air. Applause for Mrs. Lemantha's escape from a probable bite, as well as for her remarkable Ode. This applause, however, came from old men and young boys. Young marrying men did not believe in a woman speaking upon an elevated box; the Susans, Marys and 'Lizas they were about to marry had no talent that way, and they were glad on't. "Perhaps," they reasoned, "if a collection had been taken up to send these other girls a 'term' to the Francestown Academy, as had been done for the Baptist minister's daughter, they too might have been able to write Odes, and make spectacles of themselves, and occupy men's places—perhaps they would?" And thus with a leaven of jealousy, envy and doggedness, the young men never clapped a hand nor made a sign of demonstration, unless great moodiness of aspect might be deemed such.

Young men were not alone in their disapproval. The throng of women in general turned their contemptuous gaze from Mrs. Lemantha to each other, and all laughed in concert at her unlucky step upon the sleeping dog. "Mrs. Lemantha Billings needn't put on airs because she is a lawyer's wife, and don't have to milk, and make butter and cheese. She's no better than the rest, nor so smart," was their mental conclusions. "She never writ it—never!" said Mrs. Craft to Mrs. Cox, thinking the Ode betrayed exceeding ability. "Not a word of it; she can't impose on us; haint we known Lemantha Reubens ever since she was born? her husband writ it!" To which Mrs. Dow, with an astonishing toss of her head, replied:

"He write it? don't believe it; he don't know nothing much either—bet they stole it from a book."

And Mrs. Dow's opinion was the generally prevailing one. People ignorant, unacquainted with authors, have an opinion of them as they have of angels. They must be superior and invisible. The moment they come down from their height, and are seen walking upon this mundane sphere, eating and drinking like the common herd, they are suspected, often treated ignominiously, as if pretending to what they are not.

"Vain coxcomb," says the ignoramus. "Just as if he could make books, any more'n the rest of us;" and he looks him down into the dust.

Lawyer Billings had lived in a city; to him feminine orators were no new inventions. And he had not dreamed that, instead of adding to his popularity, this bringing out of his wife upon the stage was the most impolitic move he could have made.

He could not fail to see that, upon this occasion, she had failed. She had not heeded his reiterated injunctions to raise her voice; she had persisted in her sing-song; she had stepped clumsily down upon the dog!

Our young friends in the phaeton would have remained upon the verge of spectators, still occupying their vehicle; but this was not permitted.

Mr. Billings whispered to Dr. Buncombe to invite them up amongst the dignitaries and orators of the day. Rather against their preference, they accepted politely the kindness offered, therefore had full benefit of the Ode, and all that came thereafter. Ethel, flowing over with fun, looked the very imp of mischief. Vainly she tried to catch the eye of Francisco; he had learned her too well to trust himself with a glance at her face; for he would be polite, and would avoid an explosion.

Ethel's patience was exhausted, and her mirth converted into frowns, ere partaking of the cold collation was announced. And now the curious became fully convinced that the strange, unheard-of word signified a feast. And they fell to, with sharpened appetites, and right good will.

It mattered not now that a woman had spoke, and her "piece had been took from a book!" Every word of the oration (and it had been a nuisance) was already forgotten forever, and all thoughts, memories and associations of the great occasion thrown aside for a long year.

Really, to the mass of people, what is an intellectual feast compared to visible stuffed pig and dough-nuts?

And since this semi-intellectual "cold collation" had been only a sort of imitation, or pretense, what marvel that the stomach was crying out against "serpents" and "stones?"

The youthful Spaniards were really hungry, but with them *chilli* sauce was a *sine qua non*. A picnic dinner without chilli? As a substitute they made use of the pepper-sauce, and were getting on finely, unmindful of the toasts that were being given by some few who always love to hear themselves talk, when the happy trio looked up in amaze at the following:

"Young Master Francisco Otéro de Willoughby, of Santa Fó! May he live to see his country annexed to our glorious Union, and to see the darkness of superstition in his own land over-flooded by the brightness of the Christian faith!"

To which, rising gracefully, Francisco replied:

"Thanks to the gentleman. May his own country and my own beloved land, as heretofore, be watched over by the God of nations, who holds, as in the hollow of His hand, il Americana—il Mexicana!"

The youthful foreigner sat down amidst a storm of applause. There was clapping of hands, thumping of canes, rattling of glasses, huzzahs and hurrahs, deafening and protracted. Young men smilingly looked upon him with surprise, and young women with admiration. More than one matron dropped her baby to give palmal acclamation, and hands of juveniles looked as if fresh from schoolmaster's ferule.

Such a thrilling voice! Every syllable had been slowly and distinctly uttered, and with what grace of manner, what musical cadence!

"Gracious! I thought they were all idolaters and heathens out in his country," soliloquized Rev. Mr. Reubens.

"A remarkable young gentleman for a Papist, upon my word," said the rector, Mr. James Ferrol, mentally.

It was this gentleman who had tendered the toast; and, too, without a thought that it would be thus, impromptu, responded to.

Mr. Ferrol had had elsewhere a little picnic of his

own during the earlier part of the day, as had been his yearly custom, and had but just arrived upon the grounds.

Inquiring who was this handsome young stranger, (though he had conjectured, seeing him with Ethel Forsyth), he was much pleased with his exterior, and from sudden impulse had called him out, as above described.

The response had not only taken him by surprise, but had charmed him. He at once made his way to Ethel, begging her to introduce him to her cousins. With intense pride Ethel complied—and this was a signal for the Buncombes, the Reubens, the Billings, and others to do likewise, until Francisco became the real hero of the day.

Ethel was in raptures. Indeed, she had been in nothing else since Francisco had surprised her feeding her chickens. Scarcely had she been able to sleep for thinking how happy she had found herself. So much pride entered into her love and admiration for her cousins. Although she considered Francisco the finer and handsomer of the two, she yet loved Beatrice most tenderly.

And now, while on this great festival of the Fourth, the *grandissimes* of Sunapee Mount came up to do them reverence, and those also of unpretentious standing, not content with admiration from afar, came forward with simple courtesy and friendly words, Ethel could have clasped every hand with gratitude for this exhibition of good will to her favorites.

"I will never forget this in them," was her mental promise.

The collation being finished, it was proposed that Dr.

Buncombe should do his oration, after which should be singing and recitations by the Sunday school. Imperious hunger had caused these postponements; and now it became evident that they were indefinite. A general stampede had already commenced. Boys, by the score, were fleeing as for their lives for more fire-crackers! Little ones, weary and cross, filled distressedly with candy and cakes, sent forth piteous cries or angry screams. Mothers, still more weary and fretful, took up their babies and walked, their little girls following, dragging along the empty baskets, which their bigger brothers (now crazy for fire-crackers) had been obliged to tote up in the morning.

In vain Mr. Billings rapped with his cane and thundered with his voice. The crowd was bent on going, and would not be staid for so small an earthquake as Mr. Billings was striving to get up.

Dr. Buncombe, therefore, thrust back into his coat pocket the address he had much labored to compose. His look was grave—nay, severe. Evidently he thought he had not been well treated. He was joined by Mrs. Buncombe, whose face, never serene, was now decidedly furious.

"A pretty way, this!" she said, jerkingly.

Mr. Reubens came up to apologize. He went no farther than "I am *very* sorry——" when Mrs. Buncombe flew at him like a tigress.

"You intended it—you did it on purpose—and you a minister of the Gospel! You may attend to your own Sunday school—I wash my hands of it from this day."

"Begging your pardon, madame——" he commenced.

"I will never forgive you, never. This is an open

insult. I will never again darken the doors of the Baptist church, if I live to be old as Methusalch. Come on, Doctor."

As if she had said enough for both, the Doctor meekly followed. So sudden had been the exodus, none were left upon the patriotic campus save the ministers, deacons, lawyer, and their respective families.

"A very nice day, but for this miff of the Buncombes," remarked Mr. Reubens.

"A very nice day, anyhow," returned a deacon who thought the Doctor and lady displayed uncalled-for petulance and anger.

CHAPTER VII.

BASIL BRAUN VISITS "BIRD'S NEST."

REV. JAMES FERROL had never married. His sister, Mrs. Mary Braun, wedded but not widowed (it was said), kept his house. She was a neat, orderly and very lady-like person; the rector could not have desired a better housekeeper.

Mrs. Braun was the mother of one son, who had reached the age of eighteen on this memorable day of Independence. By all his acquaintances Basil Braun was pronounced eccentric—odd. As example of this, he would not spend so important a day of his life with the crowd at the Sunapee Mount celebration—therefore, after the shortened exercises of his uncle's picnic at Duxbury, he took hook and line and proceeded to his favorite fishing haunts.

And who had he for companion? His faithful and loving mother. Sad-eyed, gentle woman, in whose pensive face one might read a story of woman's love and woman's wrong.

This close and intimate companionship of mother and son was commented upon as remarkable. One often witnesses a doting fondness upon the mother's part; but instead of a hearty return, the son appears to think it manly to manifest indifference; and particularly would deem it ridiculous to be accompanied by his mother on fishing and pleasure excursions.

Not so, Basil Braun—noble, noble Basil Braun. One might talk an hour of his good qualities, nor would we be so much impressed in his favor, as by this one highest encomium—" he was good to his mother."

Fathers, whose sons had gone astray, beholding this peculiar and constant intimacy, said of the boy: "There is no danger of him."

Mothers, whose pillow was wet with tears for sons who should be beneath the home-roof, but whose steps were treading unknown and perilous places, said tenderly: "God bless Basil Braun! Happy the mother of Basil Braun!"

The rector had been home for hours ere his sister and nephew returned, the latter bearing the fishing-tackle and a string of fish, the former, as usual, with an enormous bouquet of wild flowers destined for adornment of the refectory table.

The rector greeted them:

"You missed it, Mary, and you, too, Basil, my boy, in not going to Sunapee Mount. We have been grandly mistaken in supposing Mrs. Forsyth's friends from Mexico would be barbarians; they are anything else, I assure you. The boy is a gentleman, a perfect Adonis as ever I saw; and the girl, nearly the age of Ethel, I should say, though not so brilliant, and more retiring than her brother, is as sweet a little maiden as one can fancy; and the Spanish blood predominating in them only gives them piquancy and charm."

"You are enthusiastic, brother. I am pleased to see you awaken to some interest," remarked Mary.

"It is what you will awaken to, when you behold those beautiful children of the South. I had hoped you would earlier return, that we might all drive up to 'Bird'snest' and pay our respects."

"Were the ladies themselves present?" inquired the sister.

"Only the children. And, gracious, I am astonished to see how charming Ethel has grown. She has bloomed into a perfect rose. And to-day she looked the personification of happiness. Well, Basil, I suppose all these fish would be still in their native element had you dreamed the little pigeon at 'Bird'snest' would take into her head so unusual a freak as to join the crowd on Muster-Field."

"What reason have you, uncle, for thinking my movements would be at all influenced by the going or coming of any one at 'Bird'snest?'" said the boy, with a trifle of impatience in his tones.

"O, none, my boy, none," returned the uncle, very conciliatory.

This was no new thing, that of the rector bantering his nephew upon the subject of Ethel Forsyth.

True, he regarded the twain as children yet, but years would pass rapidly, and they would be children no more. In a certain picture of his fancy there was such a fitness of things, as he mentally expressed it, that he continued to dwell upon it, until it grew more and more fixed and ineffaceable.

But Basil was "odd," nor would he give in one iota to his uncle's too apparent plan.

The mother, however much she may have secretly coincided with her brother, knew human nature better than to allow her son to see that she had a thought in the matter. Besides, she was in no haste to part with this child of her heart. Surely, he might be ten years yet all her own, before claiming another nearer and dearer.

The following morning Basil made no demur to accompanying his uncle and mother to "Bird'snest." He would like a look at these paragons. If one were an Adonis, the other a Venus, he should see it at once. He could depend on his own eyes: as to his uncle's, he thought at times they saw very queerly. Even now his expectations were small, indeed!

The carriage was nearing "Bird'snest." Suddenly Basil's eye caught sight of—was it a statue of beauty, semi-recumbent beneath an umbrageous elm? At the same moment the rector's hand was laid upon the reins, which Basil was holding, signifying a halt. The rector's eye had also caught sight of this pretty vision, which now had arisen to her feet, and was slyly, but gracefully, returning the compliments of the morning.

"This is Miss Beatrice, I conclude; may I have the happiness to introduce to you my sister, Mrs. Braun, and my nephew, Basil Braun," said the rector, adding, "we have come to call upon Mrs. Forsyth and her friends from abroad; shall we find them at home?"

With an affirmative reply, Beatrice walked beside the carriages until the gates were reached.

Mr. Ferrol was not an infrequent visitor at Mrs. Forsyth's. True, he had been unable to master his great desire to have her for his wife, and had even offered himself to her during her widowhood. Mrs. Forsyth had refused him with so much frankness, kindness, and yet firmness, as had made him her friend for life, while at the same time extinguishing every hope of a dearer relation.

And Rev. Mr. Ferrol was a much better man after this second refusal than at time of the first. The conceit had been taken out of him. And then, too, it was impossible that a man of his possibilities should not improve under the example and influence of two such models of true womanhood as Mrs. Forsyth and his sister, Mrs. Braun. Mr. Ferrol could not but be conscious of how much he owed these women, who unconsciously, under God, had regenerated him.

Without any embarrassment came in and went out from "Bird'snest" the former suitor of its mistress. And why? Because he had come thoroughly to understand her perfect truth and sincerity. She had become to him as his own sister Mary; and who shall not say this was for him, a clergyman, the wisest of friendships?

Basil would have been blind not to see the transformation, we had almost said transfiguration, in face of Ethel. Just as plainly he saw how filled with devotion was she for her cousin Francisco. This, far from exciting his jealousy, quite pleased him. He hoped his uncle would observe the same, and henceforth leave him in peace as to Ethel. He liked her well enough, but would not be forced to like her better than was his own will and pleasure.

But Beatrice, as seen so beautiful under the tree! To her Basil's eyes wandered, and he was delighted when Ethel proposed a walk by the Lake; for, as he had supposed, she assumed guardianship of Francisco, and he fell to Beatrice. She was so simple and sweet: Her accent, foreign and *naivé*, was full of melody and charm. Used to the light hair and blue eyes prevalent in the North, this girl, whose eyes and hair were like the midnight, and whose brow and chin were like the sculptured marble he had seen in New York studios, completely bewildered and entranced him.

And Basil—poor Basil, for the first time wished that he were handsome; wished that he had all beauty of mind and person, and all that woman loves of luxuriant wealth, that he might fling all at this darling Spanish maiden's feet.

CHAPTER VIII.

THE NAME OF BASIL BRAUN.

WHILE Mr. Ferrol was conversing with his hostess, his sister engaged in discourse with Mrs. Willoughby. These two ladies could but be mutually attractive. There was in the circumstances of both that pensive expression, that resigned, patient look, which is seen in faces of those who have battled with sorrow, and whose souls carry wounds and scars, until they put off this mortality.

Their words at length drifted to their children.

"Basil? Do I understand—you call your son Basil—Basil Braun?" questioned Mrs. Willoughby, with apparent interest.

Being answered in the affirmative, that lady continued:

"Have you relatives in the South—did your husband have relatives of his own name?"

Mrs. Braun became visibly affected. She blushed, attempted to speak, stammered.

"Pardon me," hastened Mrs. Willoughby to say. "I thought it possible—but of course I am mistaken—there are many names alike in the world; but Basil Braun appeared to me an odd name; I was struck by it—it was the name of a friend of my husband's—but, pardon me, you are not well;" and, rising, she offered a fan to the lady.

"The morning is very sultry, I think," Mrs. Braun whispered faintly.

Here came a proposition from Mr. Ferrol to take a stroll among the flowers, and crossing the veranda, where all were sitting, he offered his arm to the stranger, leaving Mrs. Forsyth to his sister.

"My dear, are you ill?" spake Mrs. Forsyth to her most valued friend, the rector's sister. "Lean on me; you are all atremble; let us seat ourselves on this rustic bench."

"Thank you, I shall be better directly. Do you not know I have sometimes a palpitation of the heart? The air is very heavy, is it not?"

"I thought it delightful this morning," returned the other. "However, neither air nor aught else is agreeable, or as it should be, to one ill. Shall I not bring you a cordial? Why, I never saw you like this before!"

"It is all over now, just a little faintness," and poor Mrs. Braun smiled.

Soon she took her friend's arm, and, sauntering along, came upon her brother in earnest conversation with Mrs. Willoughby. One thought came uppermost—was she telling him of another Basil Braun? Coming nearer, however, she perceived that the subject of conversation was the luxuriance of flowers and fruit in her own warm clime; and Mrs. Braun became surprised to see the animation with which she spoke.

"She may well be happy," sighed Mary Braun. "She knows not that death is a *merciful* grief; she knows no grief like mine—that is unmerciful, cruel, ever-gnawing, never-dying."

Here Mrs. Forsyth, having left her friend for a moment, returned with a bunch of flowers known to be Mary's favorites. Amidst the dewy bloom of these fragrant flowers Mary buried her sorrowful face and remained quiet.

Mrs. Forsyth did not weary her with talking. She perceived something more than usual had affected her friend; so she busied herself by plucking dead leaves and rearranging vines, until her other visitors appeared willing to return to the house.

It was Basil Braun who first thought of returning from the Lake shore, mindful that but a morning call had been intended, and that it would be rude and intrusive to extend it beyond proper limits.

"We have enjoyed a charming walk," he averred, meeting Francisco and Ethel unexpectedly; "but all things come to an end; sweetest moments flit the soonest. My mother and uncle may be awaiting me," and leading the way to the house, the others followed.

The visitors, with many promises of frequent interviews, took their departure.

"What a charming person!" exclaimed Basil.

"*Very* charming! The widow you speak of, Mrs. Willoughby, do you not?" questioned the uncle.

"No, sir," replied the boy, drawing out the vowel to an unconscionable length.

"O, excuse me, my boy; I was stupid, indeed. Yes, the young Senorini Beatrice is very pretty.

Now Basil Braun thought: "Very pretty," tame indeed; next thing to insulting when applied to an object of such superb beauty as he had just left. He felt that cold "very pretty" like a splash of cold water, but he bit his lips and said nothing. He was a strong-souled, deep-hearted boy; he had fallen in love at first sight; but, after his first impulsive exclamation, he withdrew into himself and kept his secret—that is, he thought he did: for his mother and uncle spoke no more that day of Beatrice. The reason may have been this: that all the remainder of the day the brother and sister remained together discussing some subject with great secrecy and interest.

"You are sure," said Mr. Ferrol, "that Mrs. Willoughby understood the name: it is so easy a thing for foreigners to become confused."

"Quite sure," replied Mary; "she repeated it more than once; nor would it be likely that she could mistake the name of a friend of her husband. Equally unlikely there should be two Basil Brauns."

"That part of it is not so improbable," reflected the rector; "we must remember the world is wide, and the number of people is infinite."

"I know; but you must admit Basil Braun to be an unusual name. I remember his telling me that his father, whose name was John, insisted upon the name of Basil from its oddity. And when our own child was born my husband said, 'let us call him Basil; wherever then on earth he may wander, he will be known, if at all, as my son, for I am the only Braun bearing the prenomen of Basil.'"

"I concede to the probability; at all events it is worthy our earnest attention. A friend of Colonel Willoughby! And we have always understood Colonel Willoughby to have been a noble, an honorable man. Dear Mary, would such a man have for a friend one who could be base and dishonorable? Besides, I have ever marveled greatly how it could be possible that so suddenly, so all at once, he, in whom we had scarcely discerned a fault, could have become a demon. Perhaps, after all, you were too hasty in leaving your home and coming to me."

"O, brother, did I not have the fullest proof? Did I not see it in his own handwriting? Was not his utter silence to me for months corroborative of that which Frank Houghton wrote to Caroline?"

"And Caroline Houghton was sister of Frank; she had been your most intimate friend. And what became of her? Do you ever hear from her?"

"She went down to join her brother, and has never returned. I never heard from her after she left New York, although she most faithfully promised to write. In my great affliction I cared not for human sympathy, yet her silence was inexcusable, considering our long and intimate friendship."

"Frank Houghton," Mr. Ferrol repeated, making note of the name in his memorandum-book. "I will drive over in the morning and have a conversation with Mrs. Willoughby. Meantime, do not fret yourself. It may turn out all a mistake." And here the rector hastened to give audience to a visitor who had been some time awaiting him in the ante-room.

At "Bird'snest" Mrs. Forsyth and Mrs. Willoughby were closely engaged in conversation upon the same subject as was occupying her friends at the parsonage. Having listened to her sister-in-law's explanation of the cause which had so agitated her friend, Mrs. Forsyth remarked:

"It is singular, at least. I am not unacquainted with

the fact that Mary is not a widow; although we never converse upon the one great trouble of her life, yet her brother told me all he knew of the matter. It was some twelve years ago now that she came, poor thing, to the parsonage. She was in very delicate health for a year or so, and would see no one. At length her brother persuaded her to admit me, and she has seemed to cling to me ever since. I am her only friend outside her home. She worships her boy, and he is perfectly devoted to his mother. He is a noble child."

Mrs. Willoughby returned:

"It would not be so very strange that my husband's friend, and your friend's husband, should prove to be the same individual, or that they should prove to be altogether distinct and two. It *would* be strange, however, if this young man whom I saw here this morning be no relation to the Basil Braun whom I knew in Mexico, since he bears to him so striking a resemblance."

"Is it possible you detect a resemblance?"

"Therein is my confidence in the relationship. I had heard the name before their arrival this morning. Did not Ethel more than once promise Beatrice a *beau* in Basil Braun? Even then I thought not of the Basil Braun who had sat at my board, and lodged beneath my roof. But when I saw young Basil—it was almost as if I had seen him before. Then, I could not help speaking as I did to the mother; at once I saw I had touched upon a painful subject, and was deeply sorry."

"A sad mystery I have known to be connected with his disappearance. He had always borne an excellent character." Here Mrs. Forsyth glanced questioningly at her companion, as if she could reveal aught to the contrary.

"My husband was rarely deceived in a person. I am confident he cherished the warmest friendship and highest respect for Mr. Braun," asserted Mrs. Willoughby.

"Do you know where is this Mr. Braun at this time?"

"He removed a few years ago to the south of Santa Fé, some few hundred miles, where, since the death of his wife, he lives amid his herds and his vineyards."

"The death of his wife! Was he, then, married?"

"Yes; he had a wife, but no children."

"And did you ever see this woman?"

"I never did. They never lived much at the city, but usually a few miles out. She did not accompany him to church, nor was often seen with him. The impression was prevalent that the marriage was not a happy one. Poor woman! She met a violent death."

"Indeed! pray tell me about it."

"She had fallen in habit of drinking wine to excess. Not infrequently she had been known to have quarrels, regular pitched battles, with her neighbors, the Mexican women, some of whom are low and degraded, although not much addicted to intemperance. The affair occurred just outside her own house. She was cruelly beating a young child which she had adopted. Some Mexican women interfered, the abused girl being of their own race. The enraged American woman turned upon them with all her fury. She was one to three, and yet she was the third to fall. Two of these were picked up dead, one of them Mrs. Braun!"

"How shocking!" exclaimed Mrs. Forsyth.

"At the time," continued the narrator, "Mr. Braun was on a journey to the City of Mexico; when he returned his wife had been buried for months. Without doubt he was sensitive to the disgrace; he removed soon away, living a lonely life in the beautiful valley of the Rio Grande."

Here the conversation was interrupted by entrance of Ethel, who exclaimed earnestly to her mother:

"Dear mamma, I'm so very, *very* glad! I shall be bothered no more by Basil Braun—he has fallen heels over head in love with Cousin Beatrice!"

CHAPTER IX.

THE FOUR FRIENDS.

THE ladies of "Bird'snest," on the following morning, were not surprised when Mr. Ferrol was announced. Mrs. Willoughby repeated to him the same in substance that she had related to Mrs. Forsyth, to all of which Mr. Ferrol listened attentively.

"As you never saw the woman called Mr. Braun's wife, you cannot describe her, I suppose; but, do you know she was an American?"

"Of this I am quite confident. I always heard of her as being such; she never acquired Spanish, and spoke only English."

"And you cannot give me his exact address?"

"I cannot; but can give the name of a friend at Bernalillo who will be quite likely to know. If you so desire, I will write him."

"If you will be so kind as to do it immediately, I will take the letter to the office as I return. I am anxious to be with my sister again soon, as she is suffering much anxiety."

After some consultation as to what should be the wording of the letter, it was couched in the following terms:

Mr. Basil Braun:

Sir:—I have met in the far North a young man, eighteen years of age, whose name is Basil Braun. He bears to yourself a most striking resemblance. For many years he has been under the guardianship of his uncle, Rev. James Ferrol, of Duxbury, N. H. Reminded of you by his features and his name, and thinking if he be a connection of yours that you would like to know of him, with knowledge and consent of the uncle, I have thus taken the liberty of addressing you. Remembering you kindly, as in the past,

I remain, respectfully,

Carlotta Otero de Willoughby.

It will be observed no reference had been made to Mary, and no word as to an expected reply. As if carelessly, Mr. Ferrol's address had been inserted in the body of the letter, and Mr. Braun could reply to the writer, or communicate with Mr. Ferrol, as he might choose.

This letter was enclosed in another to Mrs. Willoughby's friend at Bernalillo, with request to forward. Having received this letter to post, Mr. Ferrol made his adieu to the ladies, with urgent solicitations for an early visit to his sister.

Already the young people had started off for Duxbury. There was to be no further full enjoyment in hunting, sailing, sauntering or fishing without Basil Braun. As there were two girls, there must also be two boys.

Ethel and Basil were friendly enough, and would have been the best of friends had they not learned, by some mysterious prescience, that they were expected finally to make a match. This sort of dim perception led to an embarrassment, which was growing greater continually; and it is not unlikely, children almost as they were, that an estrangement might have ensued, had not this happy diversion intervened. Basil had not been handsome and fine enough to suit Ethel: she had dreamed of a different hero, and, behold, he had come.

Now Basil admired Beatrice, and this rejoiced Ethel's heart, for she really did quite like and respect her old playmate and friend, wished him to be truly happy, and was deeply grateful to him for preferring her cousin Beatrice: for now, selfish little girl! she could have Francisco all to herself.

The two girls this morning rode in the phaeton, Francisco galloping by their side.

How joyous, how happy they were!

The whole world was a paradise of beauty. Birds were singing throughout the leafy groves. Insects darted and hummed across their pathway, stirring leaf and flower, adding jubilancy to Nature's grand, exulting chorus. Is youth, however, ever conscious that the present is full of happiness? Youth is hopeful, prone to look forward, and sees a brighter joy in the beautiful to-come.

Nor is this proclivity confined to youth alone. While one lives, one dreams of a future brighter than the present—of something attainable, which has escaped the grasp heretofore: until, at length, that future stretches beyond the grave, and the fond joy to be reached is one not of this world.

And yet these bright young creatures were overflowing with a sense of happiness. To the Southerners all Nature wore a new aspect. The mountains—how different! The rivulets, though under summer heats, were not dry, but cool and murmuring. Farms lay adjacent—there were no broad wastes of land, no immense plains whereon roamed ten thousand herds—but houses were near each other, and people were friendly one with another. The wealthy were not so rich, and the poor knew not extreme poverty. But these young people were not sufficiently experienced to philosophize very deeply upon the subject.

This morning was Saturday—the fifth day of the advent of the Willoughby's at Sunapee Mount.

"To-morrow will be Sunday: where is the church?" inquired Beatrice.

"The church?" replied Ethel. "Why, Mr. Ferrol says *his* church at Duxbury is the only church in all the country round about. It is called St. Mark's—the Episcopal Church. That is where mamma and I go, when we go at all."

"Do you say Mr. Ferrol is *Father* Ferrol?" queried Beatrice, surprised.

"Father Ferrol! What do you mean? Mr. Ferrol is nobody's father," was the perplexed rejoinder. Francisco came to the rescue. Being a boy, he had somehow got hold of an inkling of the sects.

"In our country, cousin Ethel, we have but one great Catholic Church. The priests are called fathers. Now, one of our priests is called Father Fiélon. We do not say *Mr.* Fiélon, as you say Mr. Ferrol."

"How came you to know all that, and never to tell me?" spoke up Beatrice, aggrieved that she should have betrayed her ignorance.

"O, we boys learn lots of things from the Jesuit Fathers, that the Sisters do not think of teaching the girls," replied Francisco.

5

"The Jesuits! You don't say you go to school to the Jesuits!" And Ethel wore a face very unlike the ordinary.

"Why not, my cousin, Miss Puritan," quoth Francisco.

"I am *not* Miss Puritan, if you please."

"Nor am I Mr. Jesuit, so do not let us quarrel."

"How odd for a priest of the Church not to be called father," soliloquized Beatrice, arousing from a reverie. No one commenting, her brother questioned: "And didn't you say that singing speaker, Reubens, has something to do with a church?"

"Mr. Ferrol would reprove you for calling Mr. Ruebens' Baptist meeting-house a church," returned Ethel, who seemed to have the rector's pet idea well impressed upon her mind.

"Very rightly, I dare say, but who shall reprove Mr. Ferrol, for daring to insist that St. Marks is the true church, and not Mr. Ruebens'."

"Not I," returned Ethel, hotly. "There's no comparison between one and the other. The Baptist meeting-house is old as the hills, and as gray as if it never had a tint of paint. It's a shell of a thing, and looks like a barn. They think it's a sin to have an organ, and they sing frightfully and through the nose. Another thing, they think it a sin to have the old house heated by a stove, so they go there and freeze, except a few old women, who carry footstones and hot bricks or planks. They are well in their way, of course" (remembering an injunction of her mother about speaking uncharitably), "but we are not obliged to admire that way."

"What is it that you admire about St. Marks?" inquired Francisco.

"O, St. Mark's is a nice little church," began Ethel,

with enthusiasm. "It is a dark brown Gothic, with gables and tower. Its pews are so comfortable, and its kneeling-stools are cushioned also. Its windows are of stained glass, which reflect such a subdued light; the aisles are carpeted, and it has lovely chandeliers, and a bell, too—all which things the Baptist meeting-house hasn't a sign of."

"Quite splendid, indeed!" exclaimed Francisco, with difficulty restraining his pony, that he may keep alongside the glowing face of the speaker.

"You may well say that; and now tell me about *your* church," said Ethel, laughingly; "which is it the more like: Baptist meeting-house or St. Mark's?"

"I have a picture in my album of the interior of *my* church, as you style it; and, as I believe we see St. Mark's spire through the trees yonder, I will postpone a description until you shall have seen the painting," said the student of the Jesuit college.

"Yes, that is Mr. Ferrol's church. I had meant to point it out to you, when, lo! you were first to spy it. I do hope Basil will not have departed on one of his fishing expeditions; nor will he have done so, for his uncle is at 'Bird'snest,' and the dutiful son never leaves his mother alone. Now, here we are," delightedly throwing down the reins, a minute later, when Beatrice at the same time cried: "And here is Basil, too!" as that youth sprang from the piazza, and in a few leaps was at the gate.

"I am so glad we are here at last, Basil; it was very tiresome listening to Francisco's and Ethel's talk about the Baptist meeting-house and St. Mark's. Ethel calls them churches; truth is, I don't expect much to see a *real* church till I get back to Mexico," complained Beatrice.

"Just as you think about that," observed Basil, disposed to great complacency upon whatever subject this lovely child might choose to touch. "Of one thing you may be sure: *I* shall never weary you upon that subject—I get too much of it myself. I intend always to leave it to old ladies and decrepit old gentlemen in spectacles and wigs."

Beatrice laughed merrily, well-pleased with this sentiment, for the present, at least.

Basil led the way to a summer-arbor which was built precisely in centre of a finely cultivated garden.

"You will excuse my mother, young ladies, she is quite ill to-day, and had just retired to her room for sleep. It is much cooler here than in the house; besides, if we laugh aloud, or speak above the ordinary, we shall disturb no one—unless it be the spiders," Basil added, casting his eyes to the vine-clad roof.

"Pity to disturb the spiders," remarked Ethel.

"They may not object to a little music—that of our voices," added Francisco.

"I was just devoutly wishing you would come," said Basil.

"Very devoutly, since that wish brought us," was Ethel's rejoinder.

"How did you amuse yourselves the rest of yesterday?" Basil inquired. To which Ethel:

"We had the gayest time. We made wreaths, and crowned ourselves kings and queens."

"Kings, or king?" interrupted Basil.

"Well I may use the plural. Francisco, present, was one, and Basil, the absent, was two."

"Pretty well for you, Miss Ethel; and what else?"

"Shan't tell you," pouted Ethel; you would criticise and demur." Beatrice, eagerly:

"We had a sail on the lake, and gathered pailfuls of water-lilies; you should have been with us." Ethel quickly added:

"Indeed you should; and I want to make a bargain with you, Basil: I want you every day to come over to 'Bird'snest,'—now will you?" "Not even Sundays excepted," put in Francisco. Basil glanced at Beatrice, who said nothing.

"Beatrice doesn't want me to make that promise," said the youth.

"Ah, no one wishes it so much as she!" volunteered Ethel.

"Perhaps she will speak for herself," suggested Francisco.

Beatrice, thus challenged, said sweetly:

"I am confident Basil needs no assurance from any one of us, that he will be a welcome visitor to 'Bird'snest' every day, Sundays not excepted," glancing archly at her brother.

"O, but every day means often in the superlative degree; how tired you will get, how bored; how you will wish that fellow could stay away. You remember that disagreeable adage about familiarity and contempt?"

"No," chimed in Ethel, "we are bound to remember no disagreeabilities;" and, as if it were impossible to remain still a moment longer, she bounded up, and with face all aglow, said:

"Come one, come all! Basil, where's your pony? Two of us on the ponies, two in the phaeton; quick choose: I choose a pony."

"Have I your leave for a pony also, Master Basil," politely questioned Francisco. "With all my heart; I will order him around;" for the young gentleman perceived at once that the phaeton would fall to himself and to *her*. What arrangement could be more satisfactory?

Before giving his order, Basil invited the friends to the veranda; brought out iced lemonade and seed cakes, and even made no advance towards an immediate departure. The Southerners wondered at this delay: but Ethel at once conjectured the cause.

Mr. Ferrol soon appeared in view.

"Now we can go; Basil, we can only just wait for you to give your mother good-bye, and with our kindest regards," spoke Ethel kindly.

CHAPTER X.

EXCITING SCENE AT RED ROCK.

NOW, to which of the hundred-and-one places will we go first, Basil Braun—General Basil is your titled name henceforth, because you are our chosen leader, and we are bound to follow you." This said Ethel gaily, already mounted upon Mrs. Braun's side-saddle, her cheeks like a rose, and her eyes blue as the blue heavens.

Aside from the fact that Basil knew every portion of the country for miles and miles around, it was but natural that he should be appointed leader. He was one of those born to rule—one of those few whom the crowd look up to, and instinctively follow. He had a grand physical nature, strong and enduring. There was a suggestion of great force in that wide brow and massive head. The brown hair was straight as an Indian's; the eyes, not over large, were a violet-blue, shaded by so heavy and black lashes as to be deemed black also. The mouth—well, it was not womanly, nor pretty, nor sweet, as Ethel had often averred, but for the boy, the miniature man, it was noble, handsome, and full of strength. His figure, too, was more strong than graceful; not that it was awkward in the least, for he was too agile for that; but the vigor and robustness of the young soul imparted itself to its mortal frame. The poet says: "Almost translucent with the light divine of soul within;" although this ethereal idea would be, in its strict sense, inapplicable to our young hero, inasmuch as he was farthest from effeminate. But his love for his mother, ah! was there aught weak in that? It was highest proof of his greatness of soul.

Shall we be forgiven for having kept our party waiting this long at the parsonage gates? We did wish you to look at them as we saw them, gentle reader, and how could this be done without a further description of the fine youth, who, having seen Ethel and Francisco well mounted, was just entering the phaeton with the prettiest, shyest of little maidens?

"On to Red Rock!" shouted he, with the air of one leading a regiment. Away bounded Francisco and Ethel, for the latter well knew the location indicated, and the phaeton, contrary to all rules of leadership, followed on behind.

Sitting beside Beatrice! Too filled with happiness was Basil to speak. So unexpected, so desirable a favor was next to incomprehensible. The silence grew, and was becoming insupportable. At length Beatrice spoke, and music itself could be no sweeter:

"It is such a pretty, lovely country you have."

"Dost think so? I am glad you like it. Do you like it more than your own?"

"Perhaps not more than my own. I love our own mountains, our sunny slopes and vales. I had little society down there. My whole life has been spent in going to the Sisters for my education. You are the first young gentleman I've known at all; my brother, too, was gone, except at vacation."

Basil was delighted to hear this: she had not then left her heart behind. He simply said:

"And where was your brother, please?"

"At Albuquérquó, at the Jesuits' College. How glad I was always for his return."

"You will be wishing to go back, perhaps."

"Well, no; just now, while I am so much enjoying this fine morning, I think I wish never to go home."

What a delightful admission! How Basil wished he could find out if she cared aught for him! He said:

"I don't see how you can give up Francisco so easily to Ethel. I should think you would be jealous."

"I might be, but for you; perhaps I, too, might wonder how you can so easily give up your old playmate, Ethel, for me; she must have been like a sister to you."

"O, I never cared anything for Ethel," exclaimed Basil unguardedly; then, recollecting himself, he added: "Except, as you say, in a sisterly sort of way; I much prefer you, Beatrice; I rather would go with you than with any one in the wide world—a thousand times!"

At this vehemence of expression the gentle Beatrice threw upon the speaker her large, liquid eyes, full of earnest inquiry.

"Would you, Basil, truly?"

"Indeed I would, and why not? You are a hund.ed times prettier than Ethel, and she was the prettiest girl I ever saw until I saw you, and the moment I looked at you, Beatrice, that very instant I loved you! And I *do* love you, Beatrice!"

"Do you, Basil!" The youthful face.of the girl was lighted up to brilliancy. Joy was diffused there so perceptibly, that as Basil looked therein he had no need to ask if his sentiments were reciprocated. But the simple, untutored child appeared to think some assertion necessary on her part, in order to show herself appreciative.

"I am sure, Basil, you are already as dear to me as my own brother, and as he prefers Ethel, so I prefer you. Isn't it very nice that it is so?"

"Very charming indeed—hurrah—and now we will catch up to those equestrians;" and having thus established himself on a firm foundation, Basil hurried up his pony, and soon came in view of the *avant couriers*.

Now, do not set down Basil and Beatrice as lovers. They were children, simply. Their sudden and ardent affection for each other was much like that between Ethel and Beatrice—just as innocent. In one sense these children were childish beyond their years; in another sense, beyond their age were they wise and mature.

Soon all came to a halt; in fact, a halt had to be made, for they were come upon an army of people.

"I thought we were going to Red Rock," called out Francisco to Basil.

"This is Red Rock; I forgot to inform you," hastened Ethel to say.

"But I see no rock, red, white or blue, unless these people hide it from view," returned Francisco.

"A rhyme, a rhyme, and now it is *my* time: The Red Rock years ago was split into flinders, and, as you must know, made excellent timbers for underpinning of houses and the crushing out of mouses; and now there is naught left but the name, which is very tame—just the name, and that's all—thus to my rhyme comes a fall."

"And most rejoiced are we all," added Basil.

"Will you tell me, Mr. General, if you knew of this camp-meeting when you marshaled us hither?" inquired Ethel, sternly

"I knew of it, my lady adjutant," replied Basil.

"Then we will have you court-martialed at once— the idea of taking us to such a place. I suppose you would have taken us to a circus had there been one."

"In lieu of a circus, which there was not, I did take ourselves hither, and for a purpose."

"What purpose, Sir Basil?"

"For our amusement. This is not a common camp-meeting. This is a meeting of the Adventists, though many of the throng are probably not of that way of thinking."

"O, that is true," exclaimed Ethel, her face brightening, "this is the day the world is coming to an end; I forgot all about it."

"The world coming to an end!" exclaimed brother and sister in a breath.

"Yes, coming to an end—so these folks think. Aren't you afraid?"

"Please hush, Ethel, for a moment, and I will explain what the grand idea is of Adventism—on the whole, though, I think I will not. Let us land, hitch our ponies, press our way among the crowd, and learn it from the preacher's own lips. Elder Stunner is to hold forth at the appointed hour. The appointed hour is twelve o'clock, when the heavens will be darkened," etc., etc.

As Basil had proposed, the *quartette* soon found themselves occupying a prominent front bench. They had been distinguished among the crowd, and some really pious Adventists had politely insisted on giving up for them their own seats.

A prayer by a low-voiced woman was just concluding. This prayer accounted for the silence prevailing—that is, comparative silence. Although there was neither preaching nor singing, there was that hum of voices, whisperings, movings to and fro, characteristic of such gatherings.

After the woman's Amen had been supplemented by hundreds of Amens, a giant among men mounted the platform, and, putting forth all his immense strength into his voice, read a hymn, which was afterward to be sung.

The voice of this man, who was the veritable Elder Stunner, went out over the heads of the vast congregation, and was echoed and re-echoed by the surrounding forest.

Having finished the reading, he repeated the first two lines, which were taken up and sung by voices multitudinous, with but little regard to correctness of time or concert. So followed alternate readings and singings till the whole hymn was gone through.

Then was a brief moment of expectation, after which the Elder dropped upon his knees, and, stretching forth his broad palms, was about to commence the *Oremus*. He prudently waited, however, until the audience had become comfortably (?) settled upon its knees, to do which "was work, was labor," so complete was the jam.

Our young people did not fall upon their knees. Ethel and Basil were not only far from being "Adventists," but had no wish or expectation of becoming such. They were simply spectators. Nor was it expected by the *sects*, as Mr. Ferrol was in the habit of designating them, that any of St. Mark's people should join in their exercises. It was an unusual thing for one of the "true" flock to be seen on a camp-meeting ground. For these four young persons to have appeared at this important last hour of the consummation of the world, was deemed sufficient miracle for proof that the close fulfilment of the prophecy was at hand. Of course, as did Basil and Ethel, so did their respective companions.

These, Francisco and Beatrice, had seen no religious worship but the Catholic. To them, consequently, the exercises which followed appeared not only grotesque, but irreligious and profane.

The prayer of Elder Stunner was really terrific. In plain terms he told Almighty God, that if, after all these calculations made upon His revealed word, the last hour was not at hand, when the Son of Man should come in His glory, then His word had mocked them to scorn, had failed, and God was not God, but an impostor.

Basil and Ethel smiled interiorly, but Francisco's knees shook with terror at the blasphemy, and the face of Beatrice grew white as death.

"Ah," thought they, as at length the prayer was mercifully concluded, "did they but know of this, the Fathers and the Sisters would proclaim abstinence and fast, and through days of penance and of prayer strive to make reparation for the iniquities thus offered to Almighty God."

But this was not all they had to suffer. The prayer was followed by a speech intended not to close until the heavens should be darkened, the sun turned into blood, and the Son of God should come with great glory.

Fain would these Spanish Catholics have taken their departure from the place unhallowed, as they would have termed it, but Basil and Ethel sat as if quite enjoying it, and determined to stay and see it out.

The preacher's oration was too awful to be recorded. It was such as to excite his audience to the very highest pitch of eager expectation. Some stood in queer garbs, called ascension robes, made for the occasion. Many assumed attitudes, some kneeling, some standing, with arms folded and eyes raised to heaven. Others bowed low the head, casting down to earth eyes not worthy to behold the glory that was expected. Others fell prostrate upon the ground at such times as the Elder, in more violent bursts, struck like the lightning and awed like the reverberating thunder.

Some awaited the dread moment in an agony of fear. Some hoped it would come, for they could not bear disappointment; they had given away all they possessed, and wherewithal should they be clothed or fed? Many had faith, simple and trusting like little children; these piously and submissively would await the inevitable hour.

Time passed. The preacher grew hoarse, and apparently angry. He beat the air with his fists; he stamped the floor; he waxed and waned; he grew weary and faint; great beads of perspiration rolled down his face.

Meanwhile, in the blue heavens, sailed serenely the god of day. The unwarned birds poured forth their melody. Red Rock brook gurgled its accustomed song. The grand forest, unfrightened, bowed not its head, but lifted it aloft toward God, who set its beginning and its ending; and the whisper of its branches, and the whisper of the earth, and the whisper of the air, was, as ever, peace—peace. Ah, how beautiful, how trusting, how obedient was Nature! Only man was here discordant!

St. Mark's bell rang out the hour—but the world

moved on. The devotees, so long expectant, were becoming utterly exhausted. They had prayed, fasted, worn themselves out.

Those who had been spectators (and there had been many besides our own), one by one, began to depart. And now followed a stream of deserters, which ceased not until Red Rock became a lonely field. And still the world moved

CHAPTER XI

DINNER AT THE PARSONAGE.

ETHEL'S party at length succeeded in extricating itself from the general mass. A full half hour was consumed ere the ponies were reached and the phaeton found to be in safety. "What a relief!" was the universal exclamation.

"Now, on to the parsonage to dinner," cried the General.

"What! your mother does not expect us?" cried Ethel, with a thrill of pleasure, at the prospect of being able to satisfy her gnawing appetite before reaching "Bird'snest."

"I arranged for dinner in the beginning—I knew what was before us," replied the wise Basil.

"That is one of the duties of the General, I believe" said Francisco.

"In the absence of a quartermaster, or subordinate of any kind. Are you hungry, Beatrice?" turning to her by his side, for they were now well under way, Francisco and Ethel having darted off ahead, as if speeding to escape the dire event, which had just failed of fulfilment. She replied:

"I was unconscious of any physical want, until dinner was spoken of—then I was all ready to sit down to it."

The talk was on a variety of subjects, but, strange to say, not even a reference was made to the exciting scenes just under observation.

Francisco and Ethel had been sometime enjoying refreshing drinks, and eagerly watching for the arrival of the phaeton, which soon appeared at the gate.

Mr. Ferrol there met them, and cordially invited Beatrice, as he had already her brother and Ethel, to remain until after dinner, which would be served up immediately.

Mrs. Braun made her appearance, very kindly welcoming her young visitors, seeming quite cheerful and gracious.

All did justice to the ample meal, mirth and hilarity prevailing.

Of course Mr. Ferrol alluded to the camp-meeting at Red Rock.

"There were more folks than I ever saw there before; more even than attended the circus. I do not see the fun they find in it," remarked Basil.

"They do not go there for fun, my boy, unless do outsiders like yourself. They are sincere and honest in their convictions, and it is a great pity they are misled."

"Did Elder Stunner purposely mislead them?" questioned Basil.

"No; I have no idea but that Elder Stunner was himself misled. He gave himself up to a study of this subject, until he became a fanatic."

"Is there much difference, Mr. Ferrol, between a fanatic and a crazy person," asked Ethel.

"We frequently speak of people being fanatics, without supposing them to be subjects for the lunatic asylum. In a certain sense they are crazy—they have the monomania . . ."

"Maniacs on one subject, that is the Latin of it," said Ethel.

"Our Church, no more than yours, Master Francisco, practices not this method of worship."

"Thanks be to God, no, Mr. Ferrol. I could never dream of a worship like that. To me it was distressing, as being not only a mockery,.but a blasphemy." And the young man spoke with a sad solemnity.

"So bad as that, was it? Well, you are the best judge. In this country we have been more or less familiar with them, therefore they do not so greatly shock us, though to me they were ever very unpleasant."

"I wonder if Elder Stunner is kneeling there yet. Only think, Mrs. Braun, when voice and breath failed him he sank down on his knees and bowed his head in his hands, and he was shaking as if by a tempest," said Ethel.

"I pitied him, indeed I did; he was so sure, and yet his faith failed him; how disappointed he must have been!" commiserated Beatrice.

"Do you not think there should be a law against such an awful thing as a camp-meeting like this of to-day?" inquired of Mr. Ferrol this young disciple of the "terrible" Jesuits.

Mr. Ferrol smiled, and said:

"Were I even to think so, my young friend, I might not say it. This is a free country, one of whose fundamental principles is that every one may worship God according to the dictates of his own conscience. In this matter one may not judge for his neighbor. For instance, the religion which you practice in your country would appear to these Adventists most strange and superstitious."

"To those who know only *this* which we have seen to-day, ours would be incomprehensible indeed," remarked Francisco, gravely.

"The Sisters will not believe when I tell them about it. I can see Sister Catherine open her eyes very wide when I shall tell her I sat with a crowd who had appointed the very day and hour for the end of the world; are we not told that the day and the hour no one knoweth, not even the angels in heaven?"

This was an unusually long speech for Beatrice, and, meeting many glances, she cast down her eyes.

"So you learn Scripture at your convent," remarked Mr. Ferrol.

"We are taught our most holy religion, sir."

"How long since the Sisters established themselves in your vicinity?" questioned the rector.

"I cannot tell you; a long, long time—my mother was educated by them," was the answer.

"Do they have many pupils usually?"

"More than a hundred, often."

"Ah! do the children speak English?"

"Only very few. We are taught to speak English."

"Is the usual language Spanish or Mexican?"

"The Mexicans speak Spanish."

"Are there Indian pupils also?"

"O yes; not often full Indian, but mixed."

"Why, you have all sorts; do the Mexican and Indian learn as readily as the Spanish and American?"

"I have heard Sister Catherine say they learn as rapidly, if their early advantages have been good."

"Have you no schools but those taught by the Jesuits and the Sisters?"

"Not that I know of; have we, Francisco?"

"Not as yet; there is some talk of the Christian Brothers establishing themselves at Santa Fé; but they are Catholic also."

"You have heard of Protestantism, I conclude?"

"I have read of it—to-day I have seen it," said the young pupil of Loyola, pointedly.

Here Mr. Ferrol folded his hands for "grace," which being said, all arose from the table.

"Ethel, how could you be silent so long?" asked Basil.

"O, Beatrice has so sweet a voice, I could be forever silent listening to it," replied Ethel.

"And our mothers! what will they think has become of us?" spoke Francisco.

"They will have no fear; I told them I should keep you for the day. Now, Basil, do your best to amuse our friends. This being Saturday, I have to confine myself to my study;" and Mr. Ferrol withdrew.

The boys strolled off for a walk, leaving the girls to be entertained by Mrs. Braun.

Very soon, however, the rovers returned with a most glowing description of the reddest strawberry-patch. Nothing would do but for all to go berrying; so baskets and tin pails were brought to the front, and away tripped the laughing party to fill them to the brim.

The berries, as had been promised, were abundant, and did not give out; but the patience and love of picking did effervesce amazingly; all voted the undertaking a bore, and decreed unanimously that it should prove a failure. How stupid to assume the labor of berrying!

they said, and forthwith proceeded directly to the parsonage.

There they set up croquet, and played vigorously for a couple of hours. Each party claimed itself victor, each therefore was satisfied.

Then came lemonade and a gay chatter upon the veranda. Then some songs, in which all joined; then a song in Spanish, wherein Basil and Ethel could but listen. And last came inevitably the proposition for home. Again Ethel and Francisco mounted the ponies, and Basil had the pleasure again of escorting Beatrice in the phaeton. An hour later Basil and his pony were headed for St. Mark's, the heart of the rider throbbing with sweet memories of the day.

CHAPTER XII.

AFTER THE GREAT DAY.

THIS same day had been quietly spent by the ladies at "Bird'snest." For the first time the sister learned that her half-brother, Colonel Willoughby, for many years before his death, had embraced the religion of his wife. This knowledge proved no shock to Mrs. Forsyth; on the contrary, she received it with manifest pleasure. She then informed Mrs. Willoughby that her husband, Paul Forsyth, had been reared in the ancient Faith—that on his sick bed he had been attended by the priest, and that his mortal remains had been interred in consecrated ground at Claremont.

From books she had since read, found in his library, she had silently taken the same faith to her soul.

Therefore it had been that she could not join St. Mark's; and Mr. Ferrol had ceased to urge her upon the point, having been apprised of the state and nature of her religious feeling. In vain had he presented to her arguments to himself incontrovertible: she overthrew them all. In vain had he reasoned that as there was no church near for her acceptance, she should connect herself with that one, which was a branch of the true vine. "It is impossible," was ever her reply.

Now, was all this a surprise to the Spanish lady? It would have been a surprise and a grief to have found it otherwise. She was aware that there were forms of belief among mankind other than the true one, just as New England was at that time aware of idolaters who worship the sun, and of heathens who bow down to stocks and stones, with no possible idea of ever being brought in contact with them.

Mrs. Forsyth's knowledge of the old Faith being altogether theoretical, she ceased not to question her sister-in-law as to the practice and discipline of the same. As one of old at feet of Gamaliel, so did Mrs. Forsyth tire not of the lessons daily given; and especially did she love to listen to stories of the gentle Sisters, of their patient lives of self-denial, of their sweet charities, tender sympathies, and loving deeds to the poorest and humblest of this world's creatures.

Nor did these little histories and eulogies strike Lois Forsyth as vain or foolish as do they many who hear of them for the first time. They filled her with love and admiration and an intense desire to behold them with her own eyes. For herself, she had known sorrow enough to wish to wipe tears from the eyes of those who weep, to bind up the wounds of those who suffer, to do something for the little ones for His sake! Therefore she could appreciate this spirit of self-denial in others— it was beautiful and Christ-like, and far more to be desired than a possession of the kingdoms and crowns of the world.

So it happened that time flew by on swiftest wings at "Bird'snest." Absence of the children was no source of loneliness. The two women, alike in widowhood, and in tender sympathy one with another upon every subject, became devotedly attached, as had become the children, to each other.

On her return, rushing into her mother's room—yes, rushing is the word—Ethel exclaimed:

"Dear mamma, where did you suppose that we spent the whole day? but just think: we went clear down to Red Rock—Basil took us down—and there we waited for the end of the world to come; but it didn't come at all—and we listened to the thunders of the famous Elder Stunner's sermon; and he said if the world did not break up and finish entirely in that hour, that he never would believe in God any more!"

"O, my child, did you listen to such an awful saying!" cried Mrs. Forsyth, startled.

"And much more," earnestly pursuing the theme. "He said fearful things—my hair stood up straight, and Francisco's and Beatrice's faces were white as ghosts— we were wedged in and couldn't get out very well— though I don't think Basil would if he could—he was our leader, and he took us there, and meant to keep us till the 'crack of doom,' if it *did* come. But I knew it wouldn't—and *we* could have told them better—for if the ange's in heaven do not know, Elder Stunner does not, nor a thousand and million Elder Stunners, do they, mamma? And we never were so hungry! It made us hungry to look at that pale, cadaverous, hungry-looking crowd. You see, they had been watching and praying and fasting for days and nights—poor things—and how disappointed they were! And for aught we know Elder Stunner is there yet, for he swore a great oath that he would not leave that platform until he should be taken up with the God of Glory. Mr. Ferrol thinks he was crazy; do you not think so, mamma?"

"I do, indeed, my child. Most sincerely do I pity his delusion, and that of the poor people whom he has misled. There are thousands in this and the adjoining towns," turning to her sister-in-law, "who have thought of little else in the last months but of this fearful day. They did not sow in spring time, therefore in harvest will they have nothing. They gave away or neglected their cattle, their farming implements, their gardens, their homes, and now what is to become of them?"

"How inconceivable that the heart of man can imagine such a thing as the hour when time shall cease and eternity begin. It is enough to know that for us that hour may come any day, and that nothing is more certain than the day of our death. Where do they get the idea?" marveled Mrs. Willoughby. Mrs. Forsyth replied:

"They profess to get it from the Word of God—the Bible."

"When the Bible expressly forbids the penetration of so solemn a secret?" returned Mrs. Willoughby.

"You do not have the Bible, do you, auntie?" questioned Ethel, who, in some Sunday school book, had got the prevailing notion in her head.

"Yes, my dear, but the Church deducts from it our doctrines. When one thinks he is wiser than the whole Church of centuries, wiser than our Lord Himself, and sits down to see what *he* can make of the Holy Scriptures, you behold a result like that you have witnessed to-day."

"A result I shall never forget while I live. I would not have witnessed it from choice, yet I am not sorry for having thus indelibly impressed upon my mind the insane vagaries of those who wander from the true

Faith; who have been given up to blindness of intellect; who have hewn out for themselves cisterns which can hold no water." . . . . Here Ethel interrupted Francisco.

"Well, begging your pardon, dear cousin mine, I did not know before that you were a minister. Is that what you are really going to be? Wouldn't it be nice to hear you preach."

Mrs. Willoughby and Beatrice glanced at the pale face of Francisco. He returned the glance, but none of them made comments.

Ethel continued: "What a fine-looking minister cousin Francisco would make; wouldn't he be admired? He would have to take you and me around with him, Beatrice, to keep the rest from captivating him. That is just what I would be, were I a man—a minister—if I could keep my face smooth long enough to preach a sermon."

"Is that all a minister has to do—preach sermons?" inquired Francisco.

"And read the hymn, and pray—if you are a Baptist —or read the service if you are an Episcopalian; there, you have the prayers all made for you—a very easy life —little work and much play."

"And you think that would suit me, Ethel?"

"It would suit me first rate; as to yourself—well, no, I do *not* think it would satisfy you. You are sober and thoughtful. Often I wonder what you can be thinking of. Do you hear half the nonsense I pour into your ear from morning until night?"

Mrs. Forsyth remarked: "He probably thinks you will soon exhaust yourself, and makes all effort to preserve his patience. Really, Francisco, you must not allow my lively child to weary you. Having two cousins in the house is a happy episode in her life, and she is making the most of it."

"I think I can defend myself, dear auntie. When I tire of cousin Ethel I will start some fine morning for the sunny South."

CHAPTER XIII.

ETHEL'S OPINION OF BOOK WORMS.

THE following morning, Sunday, a heavy rain was falling. There would be no getting to St. Mark's, even had such a thing been resolved upon. Ethel was depressed in spirits. She had awakened very early, hearing her favorite kitten miauling from the outside. Miss Kitty, honored with blue ribbon fastened with silver clasp, had been accidently shut out the night previous, and was in all this pouring rain.

Hastily arising, donning her *robe de chambre* and slippers, the little lady glided out through the library, upon which her sleeping-room opened, and rescued the half-drowned favorite.

Returning with it cuddled up under her chin, she caught sight of a figure in the bay window. Was it—yes, really it was Francisco, an open book in his hand, his dark eyes riveted upon her face.

Astonished, Ethel stopped suddenly.

"Is it you, Francisco?" she asked.

"Is it you, Ethel?" was his interrogative response.

Remembering her disheveled locks, the maiden hastily retreated, wondering what Francisco could be doing thus early in the day.

Wrapping the kitten in an old shawl, she retired again with it to her couch—but not to sleep.

Was Francisco so much a lover of books as to be willing to resign the delicious morning slumber? Did he do this every day? How stupid must he think her to be, who had boasted to him more than once that she hated even the sight of a book! Ah, he was a student! This fact accounted, then, for his seriousness and gravity. True, he could be gay; but now she fancied it must be a forced gaiety, and she felt convinced that he must have been terribly wearied with her volubility and frivolity. She did not like students. They were too dull and poky. Who would have taken Francisco to be a student? Yes, come to think of it, she believed she would have taken him for one. Not that he was dull; that was impossible for him to be; but there was an air about him—a certain indefinable air of pensiveness, of refinement, of culture, which had won her admiration, nay, her reverence.

Ethel had marveled at this, but now it was explained —he was a student.

If all students were like Francisco—but how vastly different had been the graduates of the Duxbury High School, how awkward, how unrefined! "There is only one Francisco—is there, Kitty, darling?" and resting her chin on the purring pussy's head, she dropped off asleep.

"And do you rise thus early each day, cousin Francisco, and read for hours, while we all waste our time in sleep?" inquired Ethel, after breakfast.

"It is my practice, cousin Ethel, and has been for years. The early hours are the best part of the day for study," was the answer.

"But you are having vacation now; why not throw dull books aside?"

"Dull is an epithet I cannot apply to books. If by vacation is meant total absence from books, then I would altogether eschew vacations."

"So you are a book-worm! Begging your pardon, I must say I think, that is, I always have thought, that only old and homely people should like books."

"An odd notion; and why, cousin Ethel?"

"Because young and handsome boys and girls, or men and women, should laugh and talk and be merry; they should enjoy themselves and entertain each other; go picnicing, boating, horseback-riding; make life one grand holiday—and——"

"But the sun does not always shine! What is to be done on rainy days?"

"If one *must* prose over a stupid volume, a rainy day is the time to do it. Although that in itself is selfish. One shuts himself up, and what is to become of the rest who find little or no diversion in books? How would you like a blue-stocking?"

Now this was a something undreamed of in Francisco's philosophy. It is to be doubted if he ever even read of the term as applied after Ethel's intention. Taking it in its literal sense, a "blue-stocking" was simply a stocking of blue color. What possible connection this could have with the subject in question passed the young gentleman's comprehension. Ethel read his answer in his face, which she interpreted as an interrogation point.

"How would you like Beatrice to be a blue-stocking? How would you enjoy my society if I were a blue-stocking? Blue-stockings are women, they are. They worship books. Sometimes they write them. They roll up their eyes to the ceiling, and write poetry. Often they are strong-minded, and think they ought to be men. They dress outlandishly, wear slip-shod shoes, and have holes in their stockings. Their faces are sour and wrinkled; a smile would crackle them surely. They wear green veils and shabby black dresses. Did ever you see the like?"

"Never saw one answering to your description."

"That woman that was praying when we first came upon the camp-meeting ground was one of them—that is, a sort of one; about as much as we get around here. But her's is one book—the Bible—and her hymn book, and the life of John Wesley. She has them by heart. Her name is Miss Muzzy. She preaches, prays and exhorts. She has worn the same bonnet since I can remember. If ever she gets a new dress, she must have a happy faculty of at once getting it sun-faded; although I've heard that her Methodist sisters give her their old ones now and then. You can recognize her a mile away, and would take her to be a creature just from Noe's Ark."

"You are not much in favor of that class of women?"

"I should say not. Let me be delivered from them. In my opinion, book-worms and blue-stockings should live together in the same house, and have one world all to themselves."

Ethel said this with considerable bitterness of tone, seeing the beloved book still clasped in her cousin's hand, and hastened to leave the room.

She really was expecting a detaining word from Francisco, but not one did he vouchsafe. She stood out upon the veranda, tearing a rose petal by petal. She was not so much irritated but that she could feel shame for that very irritation. What would Francisco think of her? He could but think her a barbarian and a dunce, she thought. O, if there were a person on earth whose good opinion she would be proud of, happy in, delighted with, that person was Francisco, the bookworm! And him had she mortally offended! So she feared; and she was ready to sink in the depths of her own sorrowful humiliation.

Perhaps he would never deign to speak to her again, she went on musing—never lift upon her those wonderful eyes, which she was ready to fall down and worship. And to his very face she had put him side by side with a detestable blue-stocking! Her guest, her honored, adored guest, her beautiful, most fascinating Francisco, her cousin, her brother, her friend, she had insulted in her own house—even in "Bird'snest." No, he could never forgive her—she could never forgive herself. How could she have been so foolish, so insane? She had been so happy, so gay; now how miserable was she! Were it not for her dear mother, she went on dolorously, she would go out to the Lake, that same Lake on which they had had such fine sails, and had hoped for so many more, and she would walk straight in until the water should come up over her head, nor would she turn back, but keep going, going until her sad heart and all her sorrows and shame should be buried with the sweet water-lilies.

All this time of soliloquizing poor Ethel stood still, looking at the white petals lying around her, and thinking that roses, human as well as floral, were born to be torn, tortured and put to death. What a frame of mind was this! All the study books she had ever known had never troubled her like this book held tightly in Francisco's hand. That wretched book had been the cause and object of her senseless tirade, to recall which she would be willing to sit in sackcloth and ashes the balance of her life.

"'A penny for your thoughts'—do I quote correctly?" said the musical, thrilling voice of the object of her thinking, and Francisco, from around the corner, presented himself before the dissatisfied maiden.

"O Francisco!" exclaimed Ethel, bursting into tears, and covering her face with her two hands.

"Why, Ethel, my dear cousin, how is this? What is it that troubles you—are you hurt, are you ill?"

Ethel's whole frame shook with sobs and she could not speak.

"I entreat of you, Ethel, tell me; or shall I call Beatrice, or your mother?" and he would have left her

"No, no, no," Ethel managed to cry, with desperation.

"Shall I stay, or go?" inquired Francisco.

"Stay—wait a minute," and Ethel's tears began to subside.

"What *has* happened, dear cousin? Have all your chickens fallen victims to the pole-cat, or something direful happened to your kittens, your parrot, your birds?"

"O Francisco, how *can* you? I thought you would hate me, and never speak to me another word!" moaned Ethel, brokenly.

"You did! And is this what you are crying so hysterically about?"

"And are you not very angry with me?"

"O nonsense, Ethel; are you so sensitive as all that? What do I care for all your talk about book-worms and blue-stockings; it only amuses me; it instructs me also; for whatever did I know of those feminine creatures so oddly named? never heard of them before."

"And you really forgive me all I said? for I said it real spiteful, and I hate myself—and O, Francisco!"

"What is it—anything more? Make a clean confession while you are about it."

"You will think I am the greatest little goose—O, but I believe I will not tell you how very, very foolish I was! You will despise me!"

"I could not possibly despise my cousin Ethel—in truth, I like you better than ever, since you have shed so many tears on my account—what is it now?"

"O Francisco!" was all that Ethel could say.

"Perhaps you do not think me worthy your confidence; if so, do not tell me; I will not urge you against your will," the young gentleman said in an injured tone.

"Now you will think more ill of me than before," cried Ethel, with a fresh burst of sobs.

"Indeed you are making yourself miserable for nothing. When I do not like you, and do not think well of you, I will go back to Mexico. If you care for me at all, Ethel, you will cease to grieve, wipe your eyes, and be your own happy self again. Look at me, Ethel!"

The young man took her two hands from her face, holding them firmly in his own. Ethel perforce looked up, and meeting the kindly, smiling glance above her, smiled up in return.

"All right now. Why spoil one's pretty eyes, and make one's face look swollen and red? You are out in the damp, too, and will take cold. Let us go in, imprudent child."

"But, dear cousin, I haven't told you all yet: I felt so

forlorn and wretched that I was tempted to walk out into the Lake and let the waves cover me," spoke Ethel, rapidly, impressed with an idea that in return for Francisco's unexpected kindness, she must unbosom all her faults.

Francisco dropped her hand. He was a Catholic, taught to believe that suicide was a most odious sin. He looked at her with amazement.

"You thought such a thing as that!" he exclaimed.

"I know it was most foolish," said Ethel, faintly.

"Most sinful, my dear cousin. Do you not know that you would have died in mortal sin? How dreadful! But then you did not really mean to do such a thing; you simply thought of it—was not that so?"

"You will have to think as you please; but I did not do it, and now I would not, could not think of such a thing."

"Promise me, Ethel, now, once for all, that you will never entertain for a moment a thought like that, not alone foolish, but criminal in the highest degree."

"I did not think you would take it so seriously, or I would not have told you."

"You did right to tell me—you would have done wrong not to tell me; but you haven't promised, Ethel."

The wayward girl hung her head and ploughed the ground with the toe of her tiny slipper.

"How can I promise, how can I tell what may happen in the future?" she at length said, rather indifferently.

"Look up at me, Ethel; there—have you no conscience? no fear of Almighty God, no faith in the future life, no love for your heavenly Father? How dare you, frail atom of His handiwork, have cherished so wicked a thought without being contrite of heart and making firm purpose of amendment?"

"How serious you are, cousin Francisco. You make me really feel as if I have done something awful; I know I have, because you think so, and I will promise anything you wish. I will never say anything more about book-worms, blue-stockings, nor lonely walks into deep lakes—never, so long as I live, never! Now, will that do?"

"That will do, for lack of better," answered Francisco, gravely.

"Why, what would you have? I am really serious in my promise; I lay my hand in yours and declare I will not——"

"By the help of God, Ethel——"

"There! I have thought so ever since I knew you; all these days I've thought one thing—can you guess what?"

"What? Dive into a young lady's mind and catch its ever-changing fancy?"

"It would be like putting your hand in a grab-bag at five cents a chance, wouldn't it?"

"And bringing out——what?"

"I've helped to fill grab-bags—there's lots of fun in it."

"But this is not telling what it is you have known for a certainty for these last few days."

"No? well it is this—you are cut out for a minister, a serious, solemn, regular clergyman—I think you would be grand at that; did you never think of it?"

The pale face of Francisco beamed with a flash of light. His eyes sought Ethel's, and he commenced to say.

"To be a clergyman in our Church——" when Beatrice appeared upon the scene.

"I have sought you everywhere—far away, and here

you were so near. Francisco, mamma wishes you to join in our devotions. And, Ethel, auntie says, if she and you may be kindly permitted, you too will be present. Of course, we will be delighted, so come on, please," and Beatrice preceded her brother and cousin to the house.

CHAPTER XIV.

LEARNING SOMETHING NEW.

T the close of devotions, of which the Rosary formed a part, Mrs. Forsyth requested of Mrs. Willoughby an explanation of the origin and history of that peculiar "string of beads," and what connection it had with prayer, praise and worship.

Ethel's blue eyes were wide with wonder and curiosity. She would have laughed outright, had it not been for the serious gravity of her aunt and cousins. Not for the world, after having just become reconciled with Francisco, would she offend him now. Besides, she had seen enough both in brother and sister to convince her that they had a certain something in character and disposition which she had not; and she was becoming convinced that this something had to do with their religion. Therefore, she restrained herself upon this occasion, behaving decorously as possible.

Ethel revolved mentally her aunt's instructions in this wise: "St. Dominic? never heard of him before— in the 12th century—devised these prayers for the poor who could not read, to which class belonged the vast majority of people; they were never bothered with books then—sensible, I say—and he called the prayers a chaplet of roses in honor of the Blessed Virgin, hence it was called Rosary—pretty in name, at least; it is composed of five decades, each decade has ten beads; between each decade is one larger bead, at which is said one 'Our Father;' at every bead of each decade is said one 'Hail Mary,' and often comes in 'In the name of the Father, and of the Son, and of the Holy Ghost,' and as often one crosses himself, as they call it, which I think is very pretty indeed, and very becoming to Francisco and Beatrice especially; I should believe them to be altogether pious, if I did not know how jolly they can be; and then, beads I supposed were so called from *our* beads which we wear or make use of, instead of which our beads are so called from these religious beads—the word being an old Saxon word *bede*, meaning *prayer*. This is really beautiful—I am going to learn it all, and I will beg of Francisco to leave me his Rosary as a parting present. By holding the Rosary in the left hand, one takes each bead in the thumb and forefinger of the right, going from one to the other after each *Ave Maria*, so the person who cannot read knows he has said his ten 'Hail Marys' whenever he comes to the large bead, when he must say 'Our Father,' and so on. I already understand it pretty well, and I will soon learn the whole."

Thus it will be seen that Ethel's interest was already aroused; and when the three young people were again by themselves, Ethel reminded Francisco of his former promise to exhibit to her a picture of the interior of his church at Santa Fé.

With readiness Francisco complied, bringing forth a large portfolio containing photographic sketches of various towns and beautiful landscapes. From among these he took one, and, gazing at it affectionately, kissed it with reverence. Ethel was touched.

"And do you love your church as well as that? I should never think of kissing a picture of St. Mark's. But then St. Mark's is not *my* church. I have no church. I never before thought seriously about it; but, really, Francisco, I have no church."

Ethel said this sadly and with plaintiveness.

"Poor Ethel!" sympathized Beatrice.

While Francisco said soothingly:

"Never mind, dear; my Church shall be your Church, and my God, your God; now let us look into *our* church."

Somehow, Ethel felt as though a blessing had fallen upon her, and a sweet sense of happiness stole through her heart.

The picture was presented. It was the interior of the church, and struck Ethel as being odd in the extreme.

"How unlike St. Mark's!" she exclaimed. "And it is ornamented with pictures, like a parlor; and what are all those enormous candlesticks for, perched upon that queer kind of table, or bureau, or side-board—what is it?"

The New Mexicans exchanged glances and smiled. To know nothing about a Catholic church was to be ignorant indeed.

"We took you for a heretic, cousin Ethel, but we were mistaken; you are a downright heathen, poor thing!" commiserated the youth.

"No such thing, indeed! Do I worship a calf? Do I bow down before any grand Llama? Do I throw myself beneath the wheels of the Juggernaut?"

"A civilized heathen, then," correcting himself.

"You had better be making some qualification to so barbarous an assertion; but why are pews only upon one side, and of those only very few?"

"My mother remembers when there was not a pew in the church, and I am quite sure I do, also. That is the way with most of the churches in the Old World—no pews. The floors are of stone, usually, and worshipers kneel during all the ceremonies."

"Isn't that ridiculous?" exclaimed the heathen.

"Why so?"

"When they might have cushioned pews and be so comfortable!" Plainly, Ethel was "in the gall of bitterness and under the strong bonds of iniquity." What did she know of sympathy with the sufferings of our Lord, of the practices of mortification of the body for our soul's sake, of the spirit of self-denial, of the sweet effects of Faith, Hope and Charity being wrought into the spirit, making it divine and Christ-like? How much need had she of the good Sisters' teaching, thought these children of the one true Faith.

"If we were ever thinking of our own comfort, we might forget or cease to think of what our dear Lord suffered for us," said Beatrice, softly. Ethel was touched.

"I must be very wicked. I know nothing about any feeling of this kind. You must tell me, Francisco. Please begin and tell me all about your church first; this picture, I mean—what is its name?"

"Our church is called St. Francis'; named for one of the great saints who bear that name, of which there were three. A statue of him is in a niche behind the altar. This, which you could not make out, is the altar. You know Latin—what is the derivation of the word altar?"

Reflecting a moment, Ethel answered:

"*Altus—a—um* is high, lofty · that is all I know."

"And what is table?"

"Table? Virgil speaks about the tables—*ara?*"

"Yes; *altus—ara*—dropping the last syllable of each word we have altar, with us a dear, sacred word. And this is the high table, the altar upon which perpetually reposes, day and night our Lord, the dear Christ."

Ethel here said:

"It is all Greek to me; but go on explaining the picture, and then come back to all these things: what *are* all those candlesticks for?"

"To support the candles, which burn during the ceremonies of the Holy Mass."

"Do you have service in the night?"

"Mass is said in the morning, before the hour of noon."

"Why, then, have lights; are the churches kept dark?"

"Have you never read the early history of the Church. Fearful persecutions by pagan emperors, when Christians were forbidden to practice their religion under penalty of torture and death? Have you never read of the Catacombs?"

"Catacombs were subterranean places where the early Christians held meetings; I know that, and nothing more, about Catacombs," spoke Ethel, frankly.

"Well, if they were under ground they were totally dark; therefore the Christians formed the habit of burning candles, and they became so accustomed to behold them upon the altar that, when free to hold worship above ground, they still kept their candles burning. They considered them an emblem of the light which the Gospel had spread throughout the world; also typical of the light of faith in the soul, which should burn with steady splendor, flooding the joy of this world in the hearts, or brightening the grief and the woe that too often befall. An altar without lights! What glory, what life would be wanting!"

Ethel gazed into his glowing face, saying:

"Why, you know all about it; how did you ever learn so much—but it is quite interesting—see, are those vases of flowers standing betwixt the candles?"

"Yes, flowers. Our sweetest flowers are for the altars of our Blessed Lord and His sweet Mother."

"And do you really worship Jesus Christ as well as Mary?"

"Can you be serious in such a question?" and Ethel saw from the faces before her, as well as from this gravely uttered question of Francisco, that she had been falsely informed upon this point.

"I have been told by my governess, and read it in Sunday-school books, that Catholics worship the Virgin Mary—that she is their God." Ethel was scarcely prepared for the shock which this speech caused her listeners.

"It is wickedly false. It is a cruel and malignant slander upon our holy religion. Any one who knows anything at all of us, knows better. Why, we are forbidden to worship any creature. Mary, Mother of Christ, is the creature of Almighty God's hand. To worship Mary would be blasphemous. But we pay our devotions to her and reverence her."

"But this very morning, in the Rosary, you pray ten times to Mary, where you pray only once to God."

Francisco was startled. He at once saw, as never before, how a heretic, observing nothing of the religion but the Rosary, might be misled. However, his thorough understanding of the faith that was in him led him to say:

"The Rosary is a special devotion to the Immaculate Mother of God. It detracts nothing from the worship we pay to Father, Son, and Holy Ghost. It is an *aside* of our devotions, paid to Mary as being in herself sinless, and the beloved of the Father, and the Mother of the Son, and is reflected upon the Person of the Blessed Trinity, and supposed to be to Them grateful, inasmuch as Mary is to Them so dear. When one loves and honors your mother, do you not receive pleasure and honor also?"

"And so you have *her* picture hung upon one side of the altar; and who is that upon the other?"

"That is St. Joseph, the foster-father of our Lord. You see, over the altar, upon the centre, is the cross upon which is represented our Saviour—His Blessed Mother upon the right, because she is supposed to be at His right hand in heaven."

"And what are these pictures here and there, all around?"

"They are called 'Stations of the Cross.' They represent the sad journey of Jesus Christ to Mount Calvary. There are fourteen of these 'Stations.' The first is 'His Condemnation;' second, 'Carrying His Cross;' third, 'His Falling Beneath the Cross;' fourth, 'Meeting His Mother;' fifth, 'Simon of Cyrene Assists Jesus in Carrying His Cross,' and so on; 'Veronica Wiping His Face;' 'His Second Fall Under the Cross;' 'His Speech to the Holy Women Who Follow Him;'

'His Third Fall;' 'He is Divested of His Garments;' 'He is Nailed to the Cross;' 'He Expires on the Cross;' 'He is Taken Down From the Cross;' and lastly, the fourteenth picture represents His body laid in the sepulchre. A procession is formed, often led by the priests, who go through with these 'Stations' as if, indeed, they were following Jesus to Calvary. Before each picture, as they come to it, all kneel, saying, 'We adore and bless Thee, O Christ.' Then meditations and prayers are read by the priests, in which all join. It is a solemn and affecting devotion."

"Then you *do* worship Christ?"

"With all that fervor and devotion which only a Catholic can comprehend, do we worship our Divine Lord."

Ethel studied her cousin's face, pondering all these things in her heart. She had implicit faith in Francisco's word. She saw that he believed with all his heart. She knew there was that in his religion of which she had never dreamed, and she became conscious of a sudden interest to know more of it.

Beatrice sat silent and demure, like a gentle nun, quite confident in her brother's ability to give clear and explicit replies.

"You haven't told me all about there being so few pews. Do the other people stand?"

"Except when the Gospel is being read all kneel upon the floor. There is a floor now, though but a short time ago it was the bare ground."

"And people knelt upon the cold ground, soiling their clothes and getting colds and rheumatism, and risking invasions of insects and reptiles?"

"The ground was hard, and every day swept."

"You mean every week, do you not?"

"No, every day. We have Mass every day, Ethel."

"And what is this Mass that I've heard you speak so much of?"

"It is a solemn commemoration of the death and suffering of our Lord. It is an oblation of praise and thanksgiving to Almighty God. It is a daily sacrifice of the Lamb Divine, a propitiation for the sins of the world. It is that clean oblation of which the prophet said, 'it should be offered always, from the rising to the going down of the sun, throughout all ages and nations.' It is the most solemn, the most full of awe of all ceremonies."

"But they do say that in all your ceremonies there is not a word of Gospel."

"Did I not tell you that our people stand during the reading of the Gospel? Do they not then have the Gospel? And they stand, thereby declaring in the face of heaven and earth that they will walk faithfully in that way prescribed by this holy Gospel."

"I said you were cut out for a minister. There is no possible doubt of it. You will make a splendid preacher. You have made a good beginning by preaching to me. We thought there were nothing but heathens down in your country. We had thought to make Christians of you; and lo! you prove missionaries to us benighted.

"But we do not see all of your church's interior. There appear to be niches at these two sides."

"Yes; the church is built in form of a cross. We see only the main part; the greater portion of the two arms of the cross are not here visible. In each are two beautiful altars—one called the Blessed Virgin's, the other St. Francis'. Upon the right are full-length images of the Blessed Virgin, one as she may have appeared, journeying over the mountains to visit her cousin Elizabeth; the other represents her as the '*Mater Dolorosa*'—Mother of Sorrows—as she was, after tne Passion of her Divine Son."

"What is the use of these images? I have been taught to believe that your religion consists in the worship of them, which I begin now not to believe."

"It is true we could get along without them. They are not absolutely necessary to the house of God. How would your 'Bird'snest' cottage look, unadorned with books and pictures? You could eat, sleep and exist; but do not all the ornaments render it more dear and lovely? If we may seek to make our own homes attractive, how much more may we strive to make beautiful the church edifice consecrated to the service of the Divine, on whose altar forever reposes the soul and divinity of the Lamb—God that was slain and forever lives to make intercession for us? And what may we suppose more pleasing to His Divine Majesty than images and pictures of saints who have found favor in His eyes?" Francisco paused; when Ethel said:

"O, do go on, dear cousin preacher, I am gaining new light, and am resolved to know all about this strange worship of yours—that is, if you will not tire of my persistent foolishness, which I cannot subdue all at once, you perceive. As to pictures, I myself almost worship them wherever they may be. My father and mother were artists; but I, who should have been born with a brush in my hand, as Mr. Ferrol says, am entirely unacquainted with the art. Poor mamma never could bear to see palette or easel after papa died—that is why;

and have you told all about the church? Look at those funny little windows, away up so high from the floor, touching the eaves, and only on one side, too."

"The walls of the church are built of adobe bricks, which are square blocks of native mud baked in the sun. These walls are perhaps five or six feet thick from the ground a few feet upward, when they begin to be of less depth. Through this thickness it is found difficult and expensive to arrange for windows; this is one reason they are inserted at the top; another is, that for many generations the natives made invasions, committing robberies and murders; it was difficult for them to enter at windows thirty or more feet from the ground."

"What tiny panes of glass!" exclaimed Ethel.

"Yes, formerly they were not of glass, but of a native substance resembling mica, though of less transparency."

"The church must be very old."

"Nearly two hundred years is St. Francis'. Mention is made of a priest being buried in it in 1694. Around the niche in which is the image of St. Francis, behind the altar, are most elaborately carved tables of stone, put up as a wall, presenting a surface as if all formed but a single piece. This reaches from floor to lofty ceiling. Near the base are inserted one upon each side, rounded oblong stones of a blue color, upon which are engraved respectively:

"'Made by devotion of Senor Don Francisco Martino di Valle, Governor and Captain-General of this Kingdom.'

"'By his wife, Maria Ignatia Martinez di Ugarte. *Anno* 1761.'

"Thus are their names preserved who caused all this beautiful old and quaint work to be done. But soon the whole ancient Cathedral is to be demolished, not by vandal, but by Christian hands. A new one of hewn stone is being built around it. Several more years will be required for its completion, but the time will come when our dear old church of two centuries will be carried out peace-meal to make way for modern pews and carved pillars."

"I think that is a shame! I wouldn't have it. I love old things dearly," cried Ethel.

"So we all do; we regret to part with the old church, but our worthy Archbishop knows best. We have three other churches—'Our Lady of Guadalupe' and 'Our Lady of the Rosary,' and last, but not least, 'St. Miguel,' which is the oldest of all. It is about three centuries since that was built."

"How can that be," questioned Ethel, "when it was only little more than two hundred years since the landing of the Pilgrim Fathers?"

"We date long before the 'Pilgrims,' dear Ethel. We are no outgrowth of Puritanism. Before Luther, or Knox, or Calvin, before Henry VIII or Elizabeth, before the landing upon Plymouth Rock, scores of years before, Spanish missionaries of the Franciscan Order braved perils by sea and land, making settlement at Santa Fé. That is, they thus named the place Santa Fé, signifying, in Spanish, Holy Faith. St. Miguel was their first church. After many years there was a revolt among the native tribes. They drove away or murdered the Spanish invaders who had followed the missionaries, including these latter, demolished their dwellings and church, making ruin and desolation everywhere. Again, however, came the devoted servants of God, rebuilt St. Miguel, the walls of which had been too massive for the indolent natives to batter down, since which the Mexicans had become Christianized, and Spanish, or a corruption of Spanish, had become the principal language."

"I do not see how ever you remember so many things. Did you get all that from books?" inquired Ethel.

"Not altogether. At college our professors give us oral instructions in history as in other things. The history of these times of which I have been speaking is mostly in manuscript only."

"Have you a picture of St. Miguel?"

"Yes; here, too, is a picture of the ancient church. It is on a hill, near which the Christian Brothers are making arrangements for founding a college. You observe it is much smaller than St. Francis'. It is now also better lighted, and has a more cheerful look. It was rebuilt in 1710, as we learn by translating the Spanish words engraved upon the beam supporting the gallery, which are as follows:

"'The Marquis de la Penuela restored this building —the royal ensign Don Augustin Flores Vergara, the servant, A.D., 1710.'"

"What outlandish names! how can you pronounce them so glibly?"

"You forget they are of my own native tongue."

"O, that is why. There are pictures in St. Miguel's also."

"Within the sanctuary hang two pictures of the Annunciation, older than the church, as they are said to have been brought over by the first missionaries with a few other precious things secured and saved by the few friars who escaped at the time of the revolt. The 'Stations of the Cross' we find in all churches. There, is not that enough for the first lesson?"

"Since you must be tired out, I will say yes; otherwise it should be no," replied Ethel, giving her hand to Beatrice

CHAPTER XV.

"A DASTARDLY OUTRAGE."

"MAMMA, I've been very good this holyday—I've been to Sunday school," said Ethel to Mrs. Forsyth at the dinner-table. "Is that what you have been doing—playing Sunday school? Very commendable," returned that lady.

"Cousin Francisco was superintendent as well as teacher; I was pupil, and Beatrice—well—she was spectator, or visitor."

"I suspect, then, according to your definition, there have been two Sunday schools, of one of which I was not too old or too wise to be a pupil," said the mother, smiling upon the young people.

"Auntie Willoughby, are you teaching my mother all about old churches, saints, images and the like? What is going to become of us? What is the use to know these things away off up here, where people are mostly Methodists and Baptists, whose highest ideas of devotion and worship are to be found at camp-meeting? Were we to present to them a picture of the Blessed Virgin Mary, how horrified they would be! But a picture of Martha Washington—ah! that is a different thing! Why is this difference, mother—can you inform us?"

"You know, my child, how all-powerful is habit. It was the aim of Protestantism to misrepresent, malign and ridicule everything pertaining to the Church. The so-called Reformer insisted that the Catholic worshiped the pictures of the Virgin and the saints. Common sense would teach us the falsity of this, would we but reflect upon the subject. Pictures and images were extensively used in the early ages of the Church to teach and assist those who could not read; for instance, how vividly is impressed upon the untutored mind the Passion of our Lord by a picture of the cross upon which He hangs in all the agony of the crucifixion! What love and veneration may not be awakened for the Mother of Christ by reading, as in a book, from the sweet picture of her face, of her sweetness, grace, humility, and all saintly virtues? So, also, of the picture of Joseph, guardian of the Holy Family; of St. John, the beloved; of St. Paul, the grand and heroic; of St. Peter, the repentant and faithful."

"You must have had an excellent teacher, dear mamma, and been yourself a most docile pupil," said Ethel, bowing profoundly.

"This is not her first lesson, dear child," said Mrs. Willoughby. "That she learned at your dear papa's bedside, years ago; she has a good memory and retains it yet. May the seed sowed then yet bear fruit an hundred fold!"

"You surprise me, auntie; and yet I do now remember having been told by mamma or some one that papa's religion was a foreign one—unlike what we have hereabouts. And it was, then, the Catholic religion!" murmured Ethel, audibly, adding: "We are born to be Catholics—that is clear enough; we are doomed, and may as well yield. In one thing I am disappointed: I thought it was a disgrace to have Catholic relations; and now I think it the greatest of honors. I would not like Francisco and Beatrice half so well were it not for their religion; I have discovered the secret at last."

Towards evening Basil was seen coming over from the parsonage. The three started from the veranda to meet him, giving him three hearty cheers. Jumping from his pony, he returned their cordial salute, most emphatically assuring them this had been the longest day of his life.

"For two reasons," cried Ethel.

"I know of a young lady, a certain one not very far off, who always knows everything," said Basil, slyly.

"For two reasons," again repeated the willful girl, heeding not the remark of the other; "one is, you had to listen to a long sermon, then to much confusion of voices, and some controversy in the Sunday school class, then to make a martyr of yourself by staying home from fishing; that is one reason. The second and chief is that you had to wait till after late dinner before being allowed to come to 'Bird'snest' to see us two girls, whom you *knew* were dying to see you."

"Dear Ethel, how *can* you," whispered Beatrice, observing the blush upon the young man's face.

"Ethel prides herself on being very good at guessing; for the sake of peace let her suppose herself in the right this time," remarked Basil, with every appearance of good nature.

"O, you are too good altogether, Master Basil. We have been engaged in Sunday school teaching here, consequently you can't think how dull we have become. I aimed to pitch a little battle with you, and lo! you will not pick up the glove."

"Very stupid, am I not?"

"As usual," laughed Ethel.

"You should have seen our crowd to-day, Francisco," and Basil turned to the youth, continuing:

"By the way, why were you not all over?"

"You will remember it rained quite heavily in the morning; although the rain did not really prevent us," returned the other.

"It takes me to tell the truth, the whole truth, etc. We are Catholics at 'Bird'snest'—*we* are; and you at Duxbury, even you at St. Mark's, are unregenerated heathens; that is the sole reason none of us went to St. Mark's. We are not sugar. We should not have dissolved by going to St. Mark's in the rain, but we should have dampened and ruined our consciences utterly. You should have come *here*, Master Basil, and listened to our preacher, who was none other than this young parson, Master Francisco Ignatius Loyola, surnamed Willoughby, which is a wonderful falling off of name, is it not?"

"From the sublime to the ——" but Basil stopped ere he had completed the quotation.

"You do well to stop, Master Basil; without doubt you remember that I, too, am the daughter of a Willoughby."

"May it please your most gracious majesty, I do remember, Lady Ethel; and Miss Beatrice, how has it been with you this day?" turning to the young lady last addressed.

"Thanks; a very quiet, pleasant forenoon and afternoon. Pleasant memories have been revived of our old home, Francisco having explained to Ethel somewhat of our church—of our dear St. Francis'—its history, age, etc."

"And Ethel laughed all to scorn," said Basil, glancing at the latter mischievously.

"On the contrary she was most docile and decorous."

"Possible? When the heavens fall we may catch larks."

"You appear to think Ethel knows not how to be serious. One can be gay without being heartless."

"You mistake if you suppose me to think thus of Ethel. She and I are old friends, always having our tilts; we thoroughly understand each other, and we never quarrel—seriously."

Basil had commenced a forward march when first speaking to Beatrice; answering, she was obliged to keep pace with him.

"You are a very gallant young gentleman to the young lady of the house, Mr. Basil Braun," cried out Ethel, who, with Francisco, was in the wake of their companions.

Basil looked backward, his bright face flashing with happy merriment, and returned:

"The best way to treat these Queen Elizabeths is to leave them resplendently alone, thus saving one's self exile, imprisonment, or severer fates."

"Hold on, my young man; Miss Ethel is under my care just now. We have been struggling to overtake you, but you seem to have wings to your feet. Why so great a hurry? Whither going? Look at my sister panting for breath. It is really too sultry after the rain to have a walk; what do you say to having a sail?" proposed Francisco.

All faces beamed with animation.

"Capital!" cried Basil and Ethel in a breath, and then they exchanged glances questioningly.

"What is it? What objection do you two see in the way?"

"It is Sunday, and we've never taken sails on Sunday," remarked Basil.

"All the wolves, bears and foxes would set up a howl; the birds would warble through their noses; the air would be unkind, and the waters so angry as to top us all into the briny deep. But I'm for going, all the same," was Ethel's conclusion.

"You have not enumerated consequences more dire," returned Basil, adding with mock gravity: "The waters and the birds and all the voices of Nature would welcome us heartily; the judgments of Mr. Reubens, the frowns and censures of Mr. Dodds and of his co-laborer, Mr. Boggs, the horror of that old maid, now Mrs. Billings, the scowls of the Buncombes, and the righteous indignation of both Sunapee and Duxbury at large—these are to be taken into consideration."

"I fear not the whole *posse*," boldly spoke Ethel.

"I do not understand. You do not mean that we may not go out in the boat because it is Sunday?" questioned Francisco.

"That is just what we mean. But it is very quiet and secluded here; I do not see what harm there would be in sailing on waters in a boat than riding in a carriage on *terra firma*. Let us go," urged Basil.

"You are sure your uncle would not object?"

"He might object simply on account of the 'speech of people.' He has a holy horror of that."

"If a thing is right, it is right; speech of people cannot make it wrong," said Beatrice, dogmatically.

"An axiom, truly," returned her brother.

"And if there be no graver objection than what will

people say, why not go? I can depend on Sister Catherine, who assures us it matters not so much what people say of us as what Almighty God will think of us. It was impossible for us to go to Mass, but we have kept the day holy, having our devotions, meditations and instructions. Now, it is all right, and according to the Church, that we take some recreation."

This independent ground taken by the conscientious pupil of Sister Catherine had its effect; the young people wended their way through the garden and across the public road, where the boat lay temptingly anchored. In a few moments she was unmoored, and, with her four lovely occupants, went floating like a thing of life on the beautiful surface of the lake, which was lit up by reflections from the nearly-setting sun.

Now, if my reader be a Protestant, he thinks a squall came up suddenly, and that every soul was drowned. He does not believe in miracles, as a rule; he scoffs and scouts them with utter indignation. But he does affect to believe that because these young people ride on the water instead of on land on this blessed Sunday, the God of days and of justice may and will disturb the waters of the lake, overwhelm these human disturbers of the elements, when otherwise the lake would have maintained its accustomed placidity.

No; this just retribution did not occur. This miracle was not wrought as a warning to others who would go sailing on Sunday. Something, however, did happen, which doubtless the unbeliever in miracles would ascribe to the intervention of Divine Providence. Having had a delightful sail, as the deeper shadows of evening were gathering, the happy party returned to the shore. All alighted, and while the boat was being secured, merry jests and musical ripples of laughter, sweet and low, to be sure, yet audible, were wafted on the air. Audible, we say—and to whom?

As the party neared the road, and but yet a few paces from the shore, they beheld a horse and buggy blocking up their direct progress. Having no idea this halt of the vehicle had any relation to themselves, they were preparing for a *detour*, when a heavy, angry voice called out to them:

"Hallo, there; you need not go around; come up and face the music; I want to see you."

Surprised, each one stood motionless.

"Who are you? Been violating the Sunday, and haven't been to meetin', I'll warrant?" was again demanded.

"Will you please drive on and let us pass, sir?" said Francisco, in a tone of suppressed indignation.

"No, I won't, till I find out who you be that's desecrating the Sabba' day," and Rev. M. Dodds, elder of the Methodist church, struck out his whip amongst the weeds as if he would fain it should reach these culprits of his wrath.

Now, Mr. Dodds, and his companion, Mr. Boggs, knew very well who were these young people. They had been discussing these very same subjects after meeting at Deacon Short's, where they partook of an excellent dinner, seasoned plentifully with cider and scandal. In fact, the main subject of Mr. Dodds' sermon was Popery, suggested, he said, by the presence of Papists in Sunapee, who are profaning the sacred soil and polluting the pious air of the hitherto holy Mount. He had waxed warm upon the subject, and had shook the thunders of his wrath from his mighty fists; the aldermanic greater part of him had become a volcano, from the mouth of which had issued fire and stones in the shape of falsehoods and bitter hate of the true Church, which had ignited to white heat the throng of gratified listeners.

Both Mr. Dodds and his valuable assistant and echo, Mr. Boggs, had continued the talk in the same strain, even into the vicinity of "Bird'snest." The calmness and beauty brooding over the spot galled and maddened them. Why did not a bolt from heaven testify to the vengeance of an angry and long-suffering avenger?

Hark! From the surface of the lake came voices! Yes; on this sacred day, when they, the two Reverends, had stood in the pulpit doing God's work—heaven save the mark!—by showing up and denouncing the sins and abominations of Popery, and filling their own souls, and those of their hearers, with hatred and lies and malice and all uncharitableness, these wicked Papists had dared to be out enjoying themselves! This was outrageous and not to be endured silently.

And though Dodds & Co., as we have said, knew perfectly well whom they were addressing (the boat being private property), they chose to feign ignorance, the better to wield their blows.

"I'd have yer to know there's a law agin deseroratin' the Lord's day, and I can have ye took up for it, if I'm a mind—and I am. Aint six days in a week enough to travel on the lake, without violating the Sabba' day?"

"Is it any worse to ride on water than on land?" questioned Basil, following Francisco and the girls, whom he was conducting, in order to get ahead of the determined "Exhorters."

"You can't come it that way," cried Mr. Dodds, starting his horse, thereby preventing their crossing. "No wonder you are conscience smitten, and would like to flee from the voice of the servant of the Lord. No, you can't get around that way either," continued the Methodist elder, wheeling around again, blockading the road from below, as he had done from above.

"By what right do you treat us thus insultingly, I demand?" sternly questioned Francisco.

To which Basil added:

"You are carrying this thing too far, Mr. Dodds; I warn you, it will be better for you to leave us alone."

"That's Ferrol's young 'un; a good specimen of a clergyman's family."

"You are no gentleman, Mr. Dodds—you are anything but a gentleman, sir," cried Ethel, who had hitherto bitten painfully her lips, to keep back angry words.

"O, and that is the young miss—the heir of 'Bird'snest' —which Mr. Ferrol would like to have as his own, and which he means to have by marrying the boy and girl one of these days—ha, ha!" and the coarse voice of the "minister of the Gospel" echoed far and near.

It now became evident to the young people that the occupants of the wagon had been drinking too much cider, or something stronger that doth intoxicate, and they were at a loss what to do.

At length Francisco said, "Follow me," and he started to cross behind the wagon. Instantly Dodds wheeled around, and with such short circuit, that in one brief second the Reverends were upon the ground. Before they could pick themselves up, or stop the flight of the horse, the "Papists" had gained their own enclosure, and sto d panting upon the veranda.

"They shall suffer for this, the double d——d Papists," they distinctly heard, together with much more which will not bear repeating.

When this was reported to Mrs. Willoughby and Mrs. Forsyth, the latter saw a meaning to those threatening words which the innocent youths had been far from suspecting. She said nothing, however, except to express astonishment at such unwarrantable impertinence on the part of Mr. Dodds. A few days after, unfolding the *Duxbury Eagle*, and seeing under showy head lines, "A dastardly attack upon two Methodist elders by a party of Papists and Sabbath breakers," Mrs. Forsyth realized the truth of her surmises as to Mr. Dodds' threat.

"You see, my dear children, how he turns it: that you frightened his horse, that you absolutely attacked him with intent to rob, or do him injury."

"That explains the mystery of the whole thing," said Francisco. "He intended just what happened. His zeal for having the Sabbath day kept holy was aroused by a desire to sue my mother and my aunt, and get damages."

CHAPTER XVI.

FATHER ENGLISH AT "BIRD'SNEST."

HILE the "dastardly outrage," spoken of in the *Eagle*, was the topic of conversation at "Bird'snest," Mr. Ferrol, his sister and nephew arrived. This visit was opportune and hoped for. On his way (for he had come at once) he digested his course of action. He had listened to Basil's story of the affair already. Lawyer-like, he would examine the other actors separately and apart, and would then know how to proceed understandingly, although in his own mind he had not a doubt but that Basil had given him a true account. Francisco, Ethel and Beatrice told the same story as had Basil. Simple and straightforward had been the tale, and uniformly alike, as if it had come from the lips of one and the same person. To all assembled, after the examination, Mr. Ferrol said:

"With your permission, ladies, who are parents of these fatherless children, I shall proceed to have a legal investigation of this whole thing. They are not to suffer the effects of these slanderous falsehoods. Those Methodist elders must take back the lie or suffer the consequences. Their hatred is toward myself as well as to the Papists; what wretchedness of principle, what absence of charity, what total lack of all that is courteous, gentlemanly or Christian in their treatment of these dear children, who would scorn to do a tithe of what they are here represented as doing! I was never so aroused or before experienced such righteous indignation." And Mr. Ferrol prepared instantly to depart.

"So soon?" said Mrs. Forsyth—"going immediately?"

"At once, madam—now. I can neither eat nor sleep until proceedings legal shall be instituted. I will leave Miss Braun and Basil, and again return for them," he added, having been requested so to do. And Mr. Ferrol's phaeton rattled swiftly toward Duxbury Center.

"I never could have been made to believe that persons of such pretensions could be guilty of conduct so contemptible. They have no respect for themselves nor for others; no regard for truth, nor for Almighty God. I am filled with amazement." This said Francisco, earnestly.

"After this we may be surprised at nothing. They may set our house on fire, as they did that convent of the Ursulines at Charlestown," said Ethel.

"And did they burn a convent—these same men?" inquired Beatrice, with interest.

"Not these men—this Dodds and Boggs—one may take them for ruffians from their names—but a convent was really burned by a mob just like these fellows."

"How dreadful! Burn a convent! It is too incredible. These are not Elder Stunner's men, are they, auntie?"

"No; Elder Stunner would not be guilty of such folly. The conduct of men like those who insulted you last night arises from their bitter hatred of your religion—hatred founded on a false knowledge of that religion. We may say they were born with that false idea; they nurse and pet it into gigantic proportions; they think of it, preach about it, enlarge and magnify, till it becomes a colossus of the imagination—a mania—a frenzy—a horror. Elder Stunner has taken the end of the world for his pet idea. Another has taken temperance—total abstinence; another brings politics into the pulpit; and so it goes. As a general thing, when no other subject presents itself, and a man is called upon to preach, he can always fall back upon one text, and preach interestingly to his congregation—that one text being the man of sin—Anti-Christ—the Catholic Church!"

"Why does our dear Lord permit it?" whispered Beatrice, pale and trembling.

Mrs. Willoughby said, tenderly: "My dear child, our Lord said His Church should be known by its being everywhere spoken against. While on earth He had His cruel enemies, who were not content until they put Him to death! Were He on earth to-day these men would cry out as did they of old—Crucify Him!"

"Really, would they?" questioned Beatrice.

"Not if they really knew Him to be the Christ?" interrogated Ethel.

Mrs. Willoughby replied:

"There is the cardinal point of the question—if they *knew* that He was the Christ. His followers possessed this knowledge through faith. The Church's enemies of to-day lack this faith, nor will they put themselves in a position to gain it. No, I will not believe that even the bitterest of our enemies would put our Lord to death if they *knew* that He was the Son of God. But they could not know it, except as did the disciples through faith. 'Blessed are they who have not seen and yet have believed.' Lacking this faith, they could not know, would not believe, and hence would array themselves with those who derided, contemned and crucified our Lord.''

As the mother ceased speaking she cast her eyes upon Francisco, who had been unusually silent and thoughtful. He was regarding her intently.

"What is it, my son?" she inquired a minute later, the girls having gone out with Basil, Francisco excusing himself from accompanying them.

"My dear mother, I have been thinking this: that I shall always thank God that I have come up hither to this strange land. It only needed this experience to influence my decision. Now I know for a certainty, whereas hitherto the way was not quite clear before me."

"God bless thee, my son, my son! Your decision gives me the greatest happiness, and, I may add, the greatest surprise. My fears are groundless, then."

Francisco did not question his mother as to the nature of any fears she may have entertained, but took his hat and went out in an opposite direction to that which his young friends had taken.

At this moment Mrs. Forsyth again entered. She said:

"Mrs. Braun is lying down; this little flurry of excitement proves too much for her nerves. The more I think of it the more am I surprised that Mr. Hartford should have admitted to his columns such an article; the fact that he has done so proves, however, that he believes it to be true. And why not? For, are not two men, whose position as religious ministers should entitle them to credence, sooner to be believed than a simple hypothesis to the contrary, or than even the testimony of our children, which is to come hereafter?"

"Can you trust to the good sense and discretion of Mr. Ferrol in this matter?" inquired Carlotta.

"There is no alternative; yes, I think he will be reasonable and just when he shall have become calm. He is unusually excited."

And so several days passed at "Bird'snest," the principal topic of conversation being this episode of Messrs. Dodds and Boggs.

Not only at the widow's cottage was this subject discussed. Metaphorically, it set on fire both Sunapee and Duxbury. These quiet towns had at length a sensation, which became communicated to neighboring precincts. *The Eagle*, Mr. Hartford's weekly, became at once a very precious, more lofty bird. Its wings no longer trailed in the dust, but it flew over mountain and plain, over cabin and spire, till it rested by every lintel and hearthstone. It brought money to poor Mr. Hartford's pockets, joy and comfort to his wife, and food to the eight hungry little mouths, which hitherto *The Eagle* had been unable to do.

The second and third numbers following the issue which contained the "dastardly outrage" were filled with articles upon the subject, *pro* and *con*, but mostly *pro*. Throughout them all was this prevailing sentiment, hinted at or openly proclaimed, that Papacy was everywhere dangerous; that under the garb of Papists emissaries of Satan were abroad, and the whole country round about would be cursed for their sake. Mr. Ferrol's pen did valiant battle, and in pith and point quite blunted all the rest. This, however, others failed to see; they could not grasp his meaning; but the shallow sentences of Reubens and Billings, the emphatic denunciations of a Stunner and Buncombe, the delectable fulminations of Dodds and Boggs, they could fathom and comprehend, because they wished to do so.

With other fitful and unusual flights, *The Eagle* flew over to Claremont, and alighted upon the table of the Rev. Father of the one Catholic church—the only Catholic church within a radius of fifty miles.

Now, Father English was the first and only priest known in all these parts. When "St. Patrick's" had been built, some twenty years before, he had been sent as pastor, and ever since had remained a faithful shepherd of the flock. This flock consisted mostly of "hands" employed in the cotton, woolen and paper mills of Claremont. These "hands," as well as the head of the church, the Father, in the first few years had experienced indignities, received opprobrious epithets, and a portion of their purgatory from their puritanical neighbors. But at length it had come to pass that they were left alone to themselves, the self-righteous passing them by on the other side. With this the Papists were satisfied, and so, for the few past years, they had lived in peace.

Father English, reading *The Eagle*, recalled to mind Mrs. Forsyth. It was he who had visited Paul Forsyth on his death-bed; it was he who had received as visitor to his house, more than once, the widow (and little child), who, in the first years of her bereavement, had come to plant flowers upon the consecrated grave of her husband, which she had watered with her tears.

Father English was not surprised, after reading many columns from Mr. Hartford's press, to find Mrs. Forsyth branded as a Papist! But who were these relations of hers from "heathen shores?"

Enough that they were Catholics, strangers in a strange, hostile land, involved in a social and legal contest with malicious enemies, and only an Episcopal clergyman to defend them, or stand by them, counsel or console them.

There are priests who would have said: "Let them fight it out. I will not involve myself in all these difficulties and this publicity."

Father English was not one of these. These strangers might be poor and friendless—they would be imposed upon, maligned, abused—and should he gather his black robe from their contact? And why should an Episcopal clergyman be their only defender? Who was this Mr. Ferrol, acting the part of a Christian father towards these, the spiritual children of Father English?

Father English called his "boy."

"John," he said, "feed well and water the ponies; then bring them around with the carriage; make yourself ready to drive me a distance of thirty miles; and Anna," he continued to the housekeeper who came in answer to his bell, "I am going away for two or three days—pack in my satchel whatever I may need; if there are any sick calls, I am gone to Sunapee; in an extreme case they may send for me. Ah! what is this?" and he picked up a letter from the floor. It was a portion of the mail which an hour before John had handed him. From several letters, this had dropped unobserved.

It was a letter from Mrs. Forsyth, enclosing a note from Mrs. Willoughby.

The priest had been invited to "Bird'snest," and came very near going without his invitation. It was all right then, anyhow. He would arrive in time to attend the Justice's court, and he would satisfy himself as to who and what was this company of Dodds and Boggs.

Mrs. Forsyth and Ethel were surprised to behold with how much reverence and affection Father English was received by his devoted children at "Bird'snest." They kissed his hand, and with bowed head each one knelt before him for his blessing. They supposed—Mrs. Forsyth and daughter—that after this reverential demonstration, it would be all his high mightiness on one side, and all silent deference upon the other.

Much surprised and pleased were they, then, when they saw all the kindness and freedom of speech, and the pleasant familiarity, as between father and children. At once they saw a friend was in the house, and they surrendered to a sense of security and peace, to which they had for many days been strangers.

After surveying Father English, and watching all the parties in their familiar colloquial intercourse, Ethel could restrain herself no longer. As her cousins had done, she went up to the priest, and, kneeling before him, said gently:

"Bless me, too, please, Father English; for I, too, am a Catholic."

"What!" he said to the others, "have you made a convert already?"

He made over her the sign of the cross and whispered the blessing, and when Ethel arose, surprised at her own courage and impressed by the trifling, yet weighty, ceremony, her eyes were full of tears, her cheek burning with the enthusiasm in her heart.

Her aunt motioned her to an ottoman at her feet, upon which Ethel gracefully reclined, leaning her head upon Mrs. Willoughby's knee, while that lady stroked with her fair hand the golden curls of the strangely agitated child.

At the first lull in the conversation, Ethel whispered: "Say, auntie, are all Catholics like you all?"

At this—Mrs. Willoughby laughing aloud—the inquiry became general, "What was Ethel's questions?"

"She wishes to know if all Catholics are like the four (or five?) in this room," said Mrs. Willoughby.

"You should come over to Claremont, where I think you will come one of these days; you should hear Mass at St. Patrick's Church, which I trust you will do soon; you will see the factory hands on their knees worshiping before the altar; you will see that they are a very rough and rude people, many of them, but you will honor them in your heart for the true, grand faith which burns in their souls, and for the love they cherish for the Child Jesus and His Blessed Mother," said the priest to Ethel. He added:

"In one essential Catholics are all alike—in faith. One sweet tie binds them together in this world and in the next. In all countries, and in all isles of the seas, however much people may differ, they worship before the same altar, whisper the same acts of faith, hope and charity, and cry unto the sweet Mother of Christ, 'Holy Mary, pray for us.' However widely asunder. loving friends find themselves, they can meet always at one hour and place—always in the boundless immensity of the Divine Heart, which they receive at His altar of love."

"How beautiful!" exclaimed Ethel.

"How beautiful!" echoed Mrs. Forsyth.

"Dear mamma, why have we not always been Catholics?" inquired Ethel.

"From my fault, my fault, my most grievous fault," repeated the mother, faintly.

"Dear child," said the priest to Ethel, "we must let the dead past bury its dead; the present is yours, at least."

And thus the conversation continued; nor was it until the arrival of Mr. Ferrol, a couple of hours later, that the subject of Dodds and Boggs was broached. And when it came to be spoken of, a universal regret arose that such a marring, jarring topic must usurp the quiet, elevating discourses so pleasing to all present.

Mr. Ferrol had done as he had declared he would do. According to laws prescribed, he had cited Dodds and Boggs to appear before Justice Towne, of Sunapee, on a certain day appointed, to answer to a charge of gross misrepresentation against certain parties, viz: the aforesaid young persons, all minors, who, instead of being aggressors on the Sunday evening mentioned, and guilty of the outrage so bitterly and falsely complained of, were, in reality, objects of abuse and attack by the aforesaid Reverends Dodds and Boggs. This examination was to take place on the morrow, the eve of which found Father English at "Bird'snest" in close consultation with Mr. James Ferrol. This latter gentleman, after having questioned again Basil and Francisco in presence of the priest, dismissing the boys, spent a long evening alone with Father English.

At length Mr. Ferrol suddenly realized the lateness of the hour. Starting up, he exclaimed:

"Beg your pardon, Rev. Father, for so long detaining you after your hard drive; also, for not sooner inviting you to return with me to my own house, which you will honor me by making your home during your stay in this county. Basil, my boy"—hearing voices in the adjoining room—"we will have the ponies," as the youth appeared.

Soon Ethel brought in a tray of refreshments, accompanied by Beatrice with a pitcher of lemonade.

"Mamma bade me say, she has a room prepared for you, sir," said the former.

"Say to your mamma, Ethel, I will take the priest with me to St. Mark's. I will bring him around some time to-morrow. Yes, he will come when I myself shall be on my way to our famous court. Be ready, all of you, at ten o'clock precisely, and 'twixt now and then dream only of victory."

Evening adieux being spoken, soon after all became quiet at "Bird'snest."

CHAPTER XVII.

THE COURT OF JUSTICE—MRS. HULDAH AT THE KEY-HOLE.

MR. JONATHAN TOWNE, Justice of the Peace at Sunapee Center, had usually a very quiet life: too quiet for his pecuniary advantage. Sitting upon his tripod in his small, dingy office, he was more often given to smoking, chewing and snuffing, and to talking gossip with some interloper unprofessional, than to weighing offences in the scales of justice. It would have been better for poor mortality had a pair of visible scales hung suspended from his low ceiling, for Mr. Towne's only weights and measures were the money and influence of his clients.

Mr. Jonathan Towne had a better-half—Huldah. Huldah was a quiet, but really strong-minded woman. She had some regard for her liege lord, but she made against him two complaints: He did not make money fast enough—this was one grievance; the other she wisely kept to herself. Huldah loved money; she had a small bag full of coins, the savings of her own hands. She had been a tailoress in her youth, and, during her married life, having no children (to her sorrow and grief), she had been the manufacturess of the finest vests and pants in the dual burgs of Duxbury and Sunapee.

She had dropped her work—though in pressing haste with Solomon Jones' wedding suit—and listened intently at the key-hole during Mr. Ferrol's first visit.

True, her suspicions were correct: the Episcopal clergyman had called for nothing in her line; still better, he would have the "case" tried before Jonathan, and *not* before Mr. Billings. For this she would have kissed his feet.

She had not stirred when Jonathan opened the door, and, being a little woman, came near being walked over by her big husband, who just now felt much larger than before, with this weight of dignity and honor.

"I know it all—you need not tell me a word," said the eavesdropper, as Jonathan's lips were preparing to open. She went on, hurriedly:

"What are you going to do? Of course you can do but one thing. Dodds and Boggs have no money; they are poor as church mice; I never did fancy them. As to Mrs. Forsyth, I don't care for her either. She always is so stuck up; though I don't forget, and never shall, whatever other folks say, how Lois Walsingham watched by me two whole nights, when everybody thought me dying of brain fever, and she was just like an angel, that she was; but that was long ago, and neither here nor there; but you know she has money— lots of it; and one don't need but one eye to see that them foreigners just roll and tumble in boundless wealth. Now here we've lived and slaved going on these almost seventeen years, and are not rich yet; and here's a chance for you (and me, of course,) to handle some of these rich folks' gold, if you only manage it—

it must be managed, you see. What do you care if those young folks *did* scare the horse of the two Elders? Horses have been scared before now, and nothing come of it. Something *may* come of this if you manage it right—if you manage it right, Jonathan."

"What do you mean by all this palaver? What kind of a crochet have you got into your head *now?*" demanded the august Justice.

"Why, don't you see how clear it is? What a fine chance to make more than I'd earn by my needle, or you by your paltry 'cases' in forty years? Don't you see?"

"No, I don't see," said the blind or the obstinate husband.

"Then it's because you won't. Are you so stupid? I wish I had the thing in my hands. I would make it bring in a cool thousand, at least."

"Explain yourself, will you, and not go, as usual, around by robinhood's barn. Just say what you would do."

Jonathan Towne said this because he had great confidence in his wife's shrewdness and foresight. She must have an idea inside all this enthusiasm.

"Well, while Mr. Ferrol was talking, it all went through my head like lightning. He would not go before Billings, you see, because he's all one with Lemantha's father, who hates Popery and all its belongings. He *has* to come to you; and how does he know but you are just as bigoted and crankety as the other fellow. You can make him believe so; and tell him, or at least insinuate, that you fully believe the story of Dodds and Boggs. By degrees you can give him to understand that you place yourself in great jeopardy if you decide

against what all know will be the popular side—that of
Dodds and Boggs. It won't be *very* difficult to get it
through an intellect like Mr. Ferrol's, that you place
yourself in peril by espousing his cause: you are liable
to lose your office, and your wife liable to have all the
vests and pants go altogether to somebody else. Then
he will take the hint; he will make you an offer, which,
at first, you will reject; he will double the amount; and
when you see he is as high as you can force him, then take
him up! What care we for Dodds and Boggs; my
father never believed in any of 'em. They all want to
make money, and they think preaching is the easiest
way—riding around with their horses! You and I,
Jonathan, have to go on foot. Aren't we just as good
as any of them? Besides, they are beautiful children—
those foreigners! I could but think on the Fourth if I
only had a son like that tall, handsome boy; or a girl
like that innocent, pious-looking, lovely little lady! O,
Jonathan, how happy I should be!" And the childless
wife lay her head on her husband's breast and
sobbed aloud.

"Don't, Huldah, don't," said Jonathan, sympa-
thizingly. "Perhaps it is better as it is; and any way,
let us consider your proposition—a very good one, like
all of yours, dear—there—there!"

With this, Huldah straightened herself up again, forgetting her sore loss and grievance, in a discussion of
the ways and means regarding the proper conduct of
this most interesting case.

On the important day in question—that of the trial
of Dodds and Boggs for malicious scandal—Jonathan
Towne was dressed in his best, was clean-shaved, wore
blackened boots, and really believed, as his wife assured

him, that he was every inch a judge. For herself—Mrs. Huldah—she had every sign of tailoring put away. Her goose, board, scissors, every scrap of list were hidden from view. With a penknife she had enlarged the key-hole (which had been useless for years except as an ear-hole), and was at perfect liberty to seat herself by the same and gratify her woman's curiosity.

Her woman's curiosity! Who says men are not plentifully possessed also of this human quality?

Mr. Ferrol was his own lawyer; Mr. Billings was for the defendants.

The dingy office became crowded, while many more remained outside than could gain entrance.

Father English had designed remaining at "Bird's-nest," but Mr. Ferrol, thinking his presence would lend dignity to their side, had pressed him to accompany him.

We need not go into particulars of the trial. As we have seen in the interview between Huldah and the Justice, the case had been prejudged. Although, we must say in justice to Mr. Ferrol, he had made no special promises. When, at length, in successive interviews, he perceived the drift of Mr. Towne's suggestions and insinuations, he had cut him short by saying:

"You shall be well rewarded, Mr. Towne, for your services. You will have the gratitude of three most estimable ladies, and the thanks of the young people who prize their word of honor and their good name above all price. You will decide according to the merits of the case."

Jonathan had construed this into all that he desired, and had confidently assured Huldah that Mr. Ferrol was an easy person to deal with, and that all would be right.

On the other side, he had been approached, not by the attorney for the defendants, but by the defendants themselves. Not that they had much doubt of what his judgment might be; but to impress him with a due sense of their influence and position, had warned him that it would not be personally or pecuniarily safe for him to dare decide against them.

Jonathan had serenely listened to their ominous warnings—to all placidly replying, "All right, gentlemen."

The court was opened with much dignity. The Justice felt that the most distinguished eyes of the county were upon him, and he must be equal to the occasion. Still more pressingly realized Jonathan that the eye and the ear of Huldah, of far more consequence to him, were within gunshot distance, and were more awe-inspiring than would have been any deadly weapon whatsoever.

After the usual preliminaries, Mr. Ferrol read the testimony of the young ladies. Then followed the oral story of the affair by both Francisco and Basil. These latter were sharply cross-questioned by Mr. Billings, who failed to elicit one word of discrepancy.

Upon unprejudiced minds the hearing of these boys must have made a deep impression.

In decided contrast to their coolness and self-possession, was the pompous, heated manner of their accusers. Anger and vindictiveness marked their every word. Even their friends, the Baptist and Adventist ministers, perceived how much more becoming and effective would be greater moderation of tone and expression. Especially did they realize this when came the cross-questioning by Mr. Ferrol.

This clerical gentleman was perfectly cool and polite, but mercilessly cutting. Apparently, he lost sight of the men and the multitude, confining himself strictly to a dissection of the testimony, as does the surgeon to his radical operation.

Messrs. Dodds and Boggs, as well as their attorney, trusting to their knowledge of public opinion and blind confidence in popular prejudice, had taken success as granted. They were by no means prepared for this legal acumen and keen penetration evinced by Mr. Ferrol. A clergyman simply would utterly fail as a lawyer, they had reasoned. Therefore, they were astonished to see the testimony on their own side torn into shreds; not worthless, but precious shreds, which completely vindicated the truth of the opposite side.

Mr. Billings was thunderstruck. It is impossible to say whether he was more affected by the skill and profound depth of the cross-questioner, or the shallowness of his clients, who were made to contradict themselves in a breath, and, before they were done with, had been made to deny their every positive assertion. So craftily was this done, the Reverends Dodds and Boggs were hardly aware of it until too late.

During the examination an old white-haired man had been sitting near the witnesses, his hands clasped upon his cane, and his chin resting thereon. He had steadily maintained this position, keeping his eyes upon the floor, as if studying therefrom, and as if the proceedings possessed for him no interest.

After a complete rout and discomfiture had fallen upon the defendants, Mr. Ferrol wheeled around suddenly, saying:

"With your permission, Justice Towne and gentlemen, I will introduce a new witness—a disinterested witness, who was on the ground at the time of this little unpleasantness: Captain Mowbray, will you give your testimony?"

The person called upon, first raised his eyes from the floor, gazed leisurely over the crowd, then stood upon his feet.

We will here leave him standing, while we make of him brief mention.

Captain Mowbray during a term of several years had been known to this people as (in New England parlance) a "straggler;" in other words, a tramp! A respectable tramp, since he was received, fed and sheltered at whatever house he might choose to call. He had evidently seen better days. He was of commanding height, good figure, and may have been at a former period good-looking; but his face was now pitted with small-pox, which rendered him ugly and forbidding to small children and timid women. His extreme politeness of manner lent credence to his claim of being of French descent. He passed himself off rather as a visitor than a beggar; and never was he known to be without money in shape of small coin; this he would toss down to children with the petition, "If you please, my little lady (or my little gentleman), bring a glass of cider, and I will give you coppers and thanks."

Captain Mowbray was, therefore, a favorite with children, and never was treated in a rude or unwelcome manner.

And will it not always be found to pay—this invariable politeness of tone and conduct?

A recent American writer notices with surprise the

gentle, polite manners of the children of the French. They are not rude, nor boisterous, nor quarrelsome. They are courteous to each other, and always especially so to their parents and to elderly people. This he says, marveling much as to the why and wherefore, since he has children of his own back in America, and would delight to have them brought up gentle and lovely like the French little ones, instead of the "Young American" style, which, he sees by contrast, is detestable.

If you are a Catholic, gentle reader, could you not have told him the reason? At home, children are taught by Catholic parents; at school, girls are taught by pious Sisters, who are never anything but gentle and lady-like; the boys are taught by the Christian Brothers, or by the Jesuit Fathers, or some other religious. These Christian teachers impress upon the young mind thoroughly the principles of Christian doctrine—dwelling upon the beauty and necessity of obedience, respect for superiors, charity and all the Christian virtues and graces. They give "line upon line, and precept upon precept"—with what result? The American writer referred to has perceived and appreciated this result, but looked not at the root of the matter, else he would not marvel.

As we have said, Captain Mowbray's politeness was as good to him as ready cash; every household expected a visit from him—never expected him to work for a living, and ever kept in store for him a mug of cider, with his favorite brown bread and cheese.

Captain Mowbray has now been too long standing as a silent witness in the case now pending before Justice Towne. It is time he should speak.

"As you are aware, my friends, I am constantly traveling," he commenced, speaking deliberately, and very distinctly. "I pass often up and down the shores of Lake Sunapee, and never without stopping at a favorite little spot of my own, in the vicinity of that charming little cottage so aptly named 'Bird'snest.' This 'little spot of my own,' as I term it—for Nature everywhere is mine and yours to sit down upon, and rest, and love—this 'spot of my own' is a mossy mound at the foot of a larger boulder, around which grow ferns and hazle bushes, and above which towers the tallest pine of the neighborhood. I obtain a good view of the lake from there upon one side, and, upon the other, of the lovely trees which adorn the grounds of the widow's cottage, the tops of whose chimneys are discernible.

"Hundreds of times have I rested on that green knoll, the rock supporting my weary shoulders, and my eyes taking in the beauties of the whole surrounding scene. On the night in question I was there. I had been listening to the happy voices of the children upon the lake. Many times, all unseen and unheard by them, I had said, 'the good God bless these children in their youth and happiness.' Somehow, my own youth was brought back to me, and all the golden past, and the faces of the dead, and the averted faces of the living; and before I knew the tears were falling upon my hands, and the earth, the sky, the lake, all were swimming around me, when I heard the wheels of a carriage, which soon stopped in my vicinity.

"I heard the voice of Mr. Dodds call out harshly to the young people about desecrating the Sabbath. My first thought was, 'Elder Dodds, it is you who are desecrating the day, by making so harsh a speech in a voice so unlike the Master.'

"I listened silently throughout the conversation, or controversy, or 'attack,' as Mr. Dodds terms it, and I heard word for word as has been repeated by the young Masters Francisco and Basil. The attack was upon the side of Mr. Dodds. The youths were as forbearing as could be expected—much more so, indeed.

"I would have gone to their assistance, had they really needed me; but I was petrified, as it were, to the spot by amazement at the unchristian attack of 'ministers of the gospel' upon a party of innocent, unoffending children—for so these blooming youth seem unto us who are in the winter of our days.

"When all was quiet again, Mr. Dodds and his companion having picked themselves up and borne themselves away, and 'Bird'snest' had again received its own, I, too, stole onward, thinking over, with indignation, the occurrence, but never thinking I should be called upon to make a statement of the same before a court of justice.

"It was not until yesterday I learned that the whole affair had been outrageously misrepresented, and I saw a word of mine was needed; although I think the Rev. Mr. Ferrol has made a clear case, even without my testimony. I bear no one any ill will. I have no prejudice for or against any person. I simply love the truth, and would have it prevail."

While Captain Mowbray was uttering his last sentence Mr. Dodds sprang to his feet. During the testimony he had with difficulty restrained himself. In fact more than once he had made interruption, but had been silenced. His face was inflamed with anger, his eyes were burning and cruel, and he held them fixed upon the witness with withering intensity. Now, he strode forward a few paces, and pointed with his extended forefinger towards the harmless old gentleman who had borne witness against him, and cried:

"He is a Papist—a vile Papist. He is a suborned perjurer. He was never on that ground at the time he falsely says. I can prove that he was elsewhere. There is a conspiracy against me. Even the beggars of the street are called in as false witnesses, who would swear away the good character of two respectable ministers of the gospel. I leave it to you, friends and brethren," turning to Revs. Reubens and Stunner, "whether I and my friend Boggs shall be here branded as liars and hypocrites, or whether—"

Mr. Ferrol here arose and said:

"With leave of the Court, I will ask the Rev. Mr. Dodds one question, viz: How many months have elapsed since he left a very stately institution of stone not far removed from the city of New York, where he spent three years of his life, not willingly, but by will of the State of New York—will Rev. Mr. Dodds answer this question?"

Mr. Dodds remained standing, statue-like, his eyes glazed, his form trembling, when, suddenly, in midst of the silence which had fallen, he fell prone to the floor, as if stricken by a thunderbolt.

He was carried out and reported to be dead. He revived, however, through the persistent efforts of Dr. Buncombe and assistants, and was borne to the nearest house.

Nothing more was to be done, save for Justice Towne to give his decision, which he immediately proceeded to do in favor of the plaintiffs.

And thus ended this famous trial, over which no one rejoiced more enthusiastically than did Mrs. Huldah, who took her ear from the keyhole, and hurried her preparations for tea.

CHAPTER XVIII.

FROM ST. MARK'S—WHITHER?

MR. DODDS, recovering from his apoplectic fit, speedily left the town for parts unknown. So blindly put had been Mr. Ferrol's accusation in shape of a question, that few gained even an idea of its import, save from its thrilling effect.

And how had Mr. Ferrol gained a knowledge of the identity of Mr. Dodds with the ex-convict of Sing-Sing?

Through Father English.

Some four years previously this gentleman, being then in ill-health, had visited a small town in Eastern New York, where a cousin of his was parish priest. From thence he could readily make frequent visits to the metropolis for gaining superior medical treatment. During his visit the house of his cousin was burglarized, as also was the church—even the sacred vessels were sacrilegiously stolen. The room of the resident priest had been chloroformed, and he might have never awakened from the deadly lethargy had not Father English (of whose presence the burglars were ignorant) been aroused by their further incautious movements.

Having become fully aroused as to the situation,

Father English instantly remembered that upon first being conducted to his room, his cousin had pointed to a deadly weapon upon the mantel, smilingly remarking:

"Here is your defence against burglars, who are numerous lately in this vicinity. It is all ready for use; be, therefore, careful in giving it a wide berth, except in case of necessity."

With revolver in hand, Father English was just in time from the top of the stairs to give a salute to the foremost of two burly men, who were just passing through the front door. A cry from the wounded man and an oath from his companion followed.

Father English hastened to his cousin's door, calling loudly. No reply. He imagined murder and all dreadful things. Some time elapsed before, summoning the housekeeper and procuring an axe, he broke open the door—when the fumes of chloroform sickened him. Rushing to the outside he broke in the windows for a speedy admittance of the life-giving air. A few minutes later, and all would have been of no avail; the insensible priest would have awakened in the presence of the innumerable throng who bow before the throne of Almighty God.

By persistent effort he was brought back to this life, astonished at his surroundings. As soon as Father English became assured of his cousin's safety, he turned to look after the burglars. A pool of blood was dripping from the threshold, where the wounded ruffian must have rested for some minutes. Blood marked a passage beyond the gates to a tree on the opposite side of the street, where a couple of horses had pawed the ground. The direction which these horses had taken was easily traceable by the same red marks.

Suffice it to say, a capture of the burglars followed, and then the trial, at which Father English was summoned as a witness. He therefore had full opportunity of studying the faces of the culprits, and the satisfaction of hearing the would-be murderers condemned to the penitentiary for ten years.

It was then easy for the priest to recognize in Revs. Dodds and Boggs the two villains whom he had reason to remember so well. He had written briefly this fact upon a slip of paper, which he handed to Mr. Ferrol; and the use this gentleman made of it we have seen.

For "good behavior" these wolves in sheep's clothing —nor hardly clothing of sheep—had been pardoned out at the expiration of three years; and here they turned up among the grand hills and simple people of New Hampshire as itinerant exhorters. Unsuspecting Mr. Reubens and really pious Elder Stunner had been grievously imposed upon by these unprincipled strangers.

Had not then the ex convicts recognized the priest? True, they had eyed him earnestly, entertaining the impression of having somewhere seen him. They had even recalled the witness at their trial; but they remembered him as more slender and pale, while this friend of Mr. Ferrol's was stout and rosy. They had become, therefore, at ease, until Mr. Ferrol's question burst upon them like a bomb. As if really demolished by that bomb, we will allow Messrs. Dodds and Boggs to slip from our story for the present.

With considerable anxiety and eagerness did the three ladies at "Bird'snest" (Mrs. Braun had gone there for the day) and the two maidens await the arrival of the gentlemen and the verdict. In no measure were they prepared for the easy victory, still less for the complete overthrow of their enemies.

At the bountiful supper there was more of conversation than consuming of food. The priest was solicited to tell all he knew about these subjects of the "dastardly outrage," and he complied by relating the whole story, which was listened to with intense interest and wonder.

"Do you not think God inspired you to come to us, Father?" inquired Beatrice, her soft eyes filled with tears.

"My desire and sudden resolution to come was unaccountable to myself, dear child," replied the priest.

"An interposition of Providence," remarked Mrs. Forsyth.

"Though, in reality, this recognition of the villains had not much weight on the verdict. We would have had the same verdict from the testimony anyhow, which was overwhelming," said Mr. Ferrol, who had a keen sense of the shrewdness and judiciousness with which he had managed the case.

"Certainly, most assuredly," admitted the clergyman of the true Church.

"It was hitting the nail on the head, giving a tremendous clincher to turn Dodds and Boggs so suddenly from ministers of the Gospel into State prison convicts," put in Basil, who could not admire sufficiently the finale of the affair.

All eyes were turned upon the youth approvingly, when he again turned to his uncle, questioningly:

"How and where did you happen to fish up old Captain Mowbray so opportunely?"

"By the merest chance he returned this way. Everybody was talking of the affair. He saw at once that he could be of use, and came to me with his statement. But, I think, even without his testimony, we would have gained the verdict. Look at the falsehoods told by the defendants in their cross-examination! Why, they did not stand the ghost of a chance. Everything was against them," said Mr. Ferrol, earnestly.

"As is always the case with those who have not truth upon their side," returned the priest.

Early on the following morning a most unusual and remarkable circumstance took place at "Bird'snest." This was no less than the most august celebration of the Holy Mass. The priest had come prepared for everything that was necessary; the library, therefore, was fitted up temporarily with an altar, upon which were placed burning candles and vases of roses and lilies.

The Willoughbys were profoundly reverent and self-contained, having knelt to the priest in confession preparatory to receiving the Blessed Sacrament.

Mrs. Forsyth and Ethel watched all the preparations with interest and profound awe.

The friends from the parsonage had been invited the previous evening as a simple matter of courtesy, without the slightest expectation that they would avail themselves of the privilege.

Great, then, was the surprise of all, and of the priest more particularly, when Mr. Ferrol, pastor of St. Mark's Episcopal Church, with his sister and nephew, appeared and really assisted devoutly at the celebration of Mass, according to the rites of the One, Holy, Apostolic Church.

What did it mean, save as appeared on the face of the fact?

Ethel was much surprised, and felt quite slighted

when the priest gave Holy Communion to the Willoughbys without deigning to notice the presence of any other person. She watched for some signal to be given to her mother and herself, at least, for did not the priest know they were about to become members of the true Church? Were they, then, to be treated as heathens? Was not her own mother as good as Aunt Willoughby, even though she herself might not be quite so perfect as her admired cousins kneeling before the altar so devotedly, with clasped hands and downcast eyes? Did she not greatly desire to become good and pious? And here, to begin with, was a great slight heaped upon her!

Poor Ethel! Often afterward, in days and years that followed, she recalled these, her envious, bitter, fault-finding, peevish feelings, indulged in at that first Mass. And with how much wonder and regret!

But Ethel knew no better. Only a convert from the sects, or from any exterior of the Fold, knows how to appreciate the inexplicable conditions of Ethel's mental state.

The grace of God had not yet touched her heart. Extreme curiosity and admiration of religious effect as unconsciously exhibited by her cousins, led and guided her present inquiries and spiritual tendencies. How very much had this child to learn ere she could pass the holy threshold of the Catholic Church!

St. Mark's recreants tarried to breakfast, after which Mr. Ferrol insisted upon taking the priest home with him.

To this Mrs. Forsyth objected.

"I have much to say to Father English. and much to learn from his instructions." she said.

"All right; so have I. In order, then, to save time for him, let us sit down together in this room, now sacred for the time; you, Mrs. Lois (excuse me), and your child, my sister and her child, and I, doubting and restless for years, let us sit down together and learn if we can find rest from the teachings of Father English."

This said the Rev. Mr. Ferrol, to the surprise but satisfaction of all.

Known only to his God had been the state of Mr. Ferrol's mind for several years. His attention had been drawn to the subject of Catholicity through Mrs. Forsyth. She had read several books belonging to her late husband, and had naturally spoken of the subject-matter to the pastor of the church where she was an attendant, though not a communicant.

In order to answer intelligibly, Mr. Ferrol was obliged also to read the books.

Studying for combating arguments, he could find none satisfactory to Mrs. Forsyth; and in controversy with her became unsettled in his convictions, and finally found himself cast rudderless upon a sea of doubt.

It may not have been a "sea of doubt" precisely. He saw what he did not wish to see, and felt what he was not willing to cherish or acknowledge. Hence the struggle, the contest, which he was pleased to term "doubt," because, through that balancing position, he was still on vantage ground, and might not go "over" necessarily.

After studying Milner and Wiseman, Newman and Manning, Wilberforce and Allies, Brownson and Faber, he turned back again and again to Pusey and Foulkes, bringing to bear upon them the strongest concentration of will and positive determinations of belief. In vain!

and he became angry at himself. He put away all books, and for weeks meditated and prayed. What result could follow after having surrendered himself to be guided by Almighty God but that the all-merciful Father and Author of Truth should bring him to Himself in His own Church?

Mr. Ferrol had not been bred in the Episcopal Church. His grandfather had been a Congregational minister, and his father a deacon in the same religious society. It is unnecessary to narrate the particulars of his conversion to that church in which he had been ordained—that church which has been properly termed the "half-way house" from the sects to Catholicity. The fact of his having gone so far toward the right made the impetus almost irresistible for reaching the goal.

Having surprised all at "Bird'snest" by this unfolding of his inner self, he was, in his turn, to be surprised when his sister Mary—Mrs. Braun—took her place also amidst the neophytes to be instructed.

She observed his look of inquiry, and to his "And you, too, Mary?" replied:

"Yes, I have read all the books also; I divined your agitation with regard to their teaching; often I wished to speak to you upon the subject, but a feeling that you would wish to be unsuspected, restrained me. I could not become an Episcopalian, but I think I would become a Catholic."

And thus the "little leaven" had been working.

Paul Forsyth, being dead, through books which he had loved and treasured, had wrought miracles for God.

Basil listened as quietly as the others, while his uncle propounded questions, and Father English readily answered them with such amplifications as were necessary. But Basil had really no pious proclivities. Wiseman or Pusey might have laid upon the table for years, nor would he have been able to say which was Catholic, which Anglican. As a child, he tossed aside the Sunday school books, wherein the hero was too good for this world, while he reveled with avidity upon those pages whereon the mischievous lad got into all sorts of difficulties, fell into pools, dropped headlong from high apple-boughs, came within a breath of being drowned, suffered hair-breadth escapes continually, and had not the slightest ambition "to die and be an angel."

Such were the heroes he gloried in; then came "Robinson Crusoe," which nearly set him wild, and "Sinbad the Sailor," and "Arabian Nights." He did not fancy "Gulliver's Travels"—the stories were too marvelous to be true; and yet, later on, "Don Quixote" fascinated him. Tales of hunting and fishing, like the "Leather-Stocking;" historical tales, as those of "Waverly," every one of which he had devoured; even Jules Verne's "Extravagances;" all had for him an absorbing charm. But as to very pious books, he had no use for them.

Basil himself was rather surprised and uneasy at this. He wondered why he was not like the few other children in his class, who were attentive at prayers, and whose minds did not run on fish-poles, and deep, shady nooks of water, while they were on their knees.

Thus for years Basil had been troubled in mind, more or less, that he was *not* piously inclined, and had been rather disposed to regard himself as unregenerate and heathen, which his uncle sometimes assured him he already was. Of later years, however, he had become quite careless as to serious religious matters. At Methodist camp-meetings he had listened to free-will doctrines; at Baptist meetings he had heard Calvinistic tenets dwelt upon; from his uncle's lips he had heard both one and the other put forward at different times as being integral truth. Being of a philosophic, logical turn of mind, he had put this, that and the other together, and, making nothing out of the whole, he let all go overboard, himself standing upon a sort of self-made ground, whose "root and fibre" was this: That while he did not lie, steal or commit murder, of which there was no possible danger, he would not be condemned to hell for all eternity.

Here was where Basil was somewhat comfortably resting—the more so for this reason:

Looking around, even upon deacons and ministers, he could detect nothing very saintly in conduct or manners; common members of the churches had nothing to distinguish them from the ungodly, except some few who spoke with a nasal twang when religion was the topic. And thus all things combined to make Basil well satisfied with the negative faith that was in him.

He had admitted to himself that he had fallen violently in love with Beatrice. He was aware that what he so loved in her was her gentleness, sweetness, amiability, which, he was convinced, sprang from true piety.

For the first time he came to appreciate and understand the beauty of a truly religious nature. True, his mother was good; but he had never regarded her as pious. His uncle would not be guilty of a deadly sin, but he, neither, had Beatrice's piety.

Here was a question for the young philosopher: Did Beatrice lend a charm to piety, or did piety lend the charm to Beatrice?

Something of this he was revolving over in his mind during the controversy between the priest and his uncle. He was not interested. He was ashamed to feel that he was even bored.

Why should they be shut up indoors, while without the morning was so inviting and glorious?

If heaven intended one always to be praying, and singing, and listening to sermons, why was he placed in a world where it was necessary to gain his living by the sweat of his brow? If a man must bow down his head like a bulrush, and go mourning for his sins day after day, why was not the world one of darkness and ugliness, that the beauty of the sky, earth and water might not tempt him to love them too well? Was not God the Father, good and loving? Did He not make man in His own image and likeness, place him in a world that was still beautiful, even outside of Eden? Was man so very wicked?

He might have recalled those impostors, the self-styled Elders, who only yesterday had proved themselves to be "in the gall of bitterness, and under the strong bonds of iniquity."

But Basil was not now in a discriminating mood. He was wondering within himself what such a company of well-disposed persons as the library of "Bird'snest" then contained could find more interesting in a dry religious discussion, than in the glorious outside, the breeze from the lake, the fragrance of flowers, the singing of birds, all which he was longing to enjoy.

All was different with Francisco. He had an ardent disposition, a penetrating mind, an affectionate heart. He loved Nature even as did Basil; but, unlike the latter, not simply because her handiwork was beautiful and challenged his admiration, but because, looking "through Nature up to Nature's God," he loved the Giver more than the good gifts. Simplicities, grandeurs, sublimities of dell, plain or mountain borrowed their superlative attraction from the ever-present idea of their omnipotent Creator. From earliest childhood he had been trained to that fine spiritual sense which made it impossible that he should not think of God in every beauty that met his eye, in every sweet sound, in every fragrance.

There are those who would assert Francisco to have been naturally religious. It is to be doubted—nay, it is to be considered certain, had he received the same training as had Basil that his spiritual nature would have lacked the refined sensitiveness which now characterized it. And yet, Francisco was not effeminate nor timid. On the contrary, he was essentially noble and manly. A fine outcome of the teaching of the Jesuits. Firm, wise and true, gentle and Christian, his religious faith was not dimmed by the shadow of a doubt. It was a part of himself, and would have sustained him through martyrdom.

Composed and attentive, Francisco listened to every word on either side. He was not so much surprised at the position now assumed by Mr. Ferrol, as he had hitherto been surprised that any human being could be anything but a Catholic. He had read of heretics, and been told of them, but it had not been in his nature to conceive how they could be possibly sincere and conscientious. Hence had he been so powerfully affected at the camp-meeting. A sort of indignation at the blasphemy and familiarity struggled with his pity and compassion.

"How much they need enlightening and instructing, these worse than heathens!" had been his mental ejaculation. He would have smiled with disdain had these heretics explained how they regarded the teachings of his beloved Church.

Beatrice's mind, too, was full of peace and comfort. Like Francisco, every emotion of her nature was subject to that higher religious sense, which rendered it impossible for her to be restless, suspicious, repining, fretful. Did not God rule, govern, love and bless? What had she to do but in all things to love and trust Him—in her weakness reposing upon His strength, laying ever upon the altar of her loving sacrifice all the desires of her heart, with a complete submission and humble, adoring reverence.

She thought joyfully: "Jesus, His Blessed Mother, and the whole court of heaven are rejoicing over sinners doing penance. I will write to dear Sister Catherine, telling her and all the other Sisters of this first Mass in the library, of Father English's visit, and all the converts about to be received into the bosom of the Church."

Mrs. Willoughby read the hearts of her children through their countenances, and her own beat in perfect unison. Mrs. Forsyth and Ethel were intent upon every word, as also was Mrs. Braun; only Basil felt himself to be an Ishmaelite.

CHAPTER XIX.

MR. FERROL'S BISHOP—CHRISTMAS AT CLAREMONT.

FATHER ENGLISH was obliged to leave for his home on the following day. He made an appointment, however, to repeat his visit at the expiration of two weeks. From Paul Forsyth's library he selected some books for his neophytes, and distributed the catechism, of which he had taken the precaution to bring several.

Basil secretly rejoiced when the priest took his departure, though he had knelt with the others to receive the Rev. Father's blessing. Scarcely had the carriage disappeared from view, when this hard-hearted youth—for such he really thought himself to be—proposed to ride to Red Rock.

"Not to Red Rock!" remonstrated Francisco.

"To Red Rock? To another camp-meeting? Why, Basil!" exclaimed Beatrice, with that in her tones which convinced Basil that she thought as harshly of him as did he of himself.

"O no! We shall find no one there but some stray cows, some innocent sheep, plenty of blackbirds, and, best of all, any amount of delicious blackberries, which are just ripe.

"O, let us go," cried Ethel. "It has been so long since we have had a fine day out."

"And it's the nicest drive in the world—the road is better than in any other direction—and then the berries, you know!" added Basil.

"All right—I am ready—bravo! a gallop will do us good; do you not say so, Ethel?" asked Francisco, turning to his cousin, having entered into the spirit of the proposition.

In half an hour all was ready for a start; a lunch had been prepared, the phaeton and pony brought around—Ethel's pony—and Basil's for Francisco; for it seemed tacitly agreed that Basil and Beatrice should appropriate the phaeton, as before.

The respective mothers came out to give their injunctions and adieus, and away went the young people, full of life and glee. They went just in time to miss the arrival of the *Eagle*, which was welcomed with interest by those left at "Bird'snest."

Mr. Ferrol being asked to read aloud any comments which might be made upon the trial and verdict, proceeded to render the following: "Justice to all parties compels us to express our deep regret for the publication, two weeks ago, of an article headed 'A dastardly outrage.' The author of that article and his companion have proved themselves villains of the deepest dye, inasmuch as, professing to be ministers of the gospel, they were arrant impostors, having stolen the livery of Heaven to serve the devil in. Instead of being attacked by the parties referred to, they were themselves the assailants, and solely on the ground of religious intolerance."

Here followed an account of the trial, which it is unnecessary to repeat, and the article closed with a eulogium of Mr. Ferrol, in which was expressed the conviction that in the pastor of St. Mark's Church had been buried talents which would have elevated him to the most brilliant height as an advocate and a jurist.

Not only had Mr. Hartford, editor of the *Eagle*, made the *amende honorable*, but Mr. Reubens and Elder Stunner had come out with an article under their own signatures, explaining how they had been deceived in men so specially unworthy of their confidence. They expressed themselves as most regretful for the sensation caused, for the injury to religion and for the injustice to innocent parties. A local item also stated that the friend who accompanied Mr. Ferrol during the trial, about whom there had been so much speculation, was the Catholic priest from Claremont. He had conducted himself in a gentlemanly manner, and no one had a suspicion that so unusual a personage had been in their midst. Thus much from the less lordly *Eagle*.

Mrs. Huldah became much exercised when she discovered that a Catholic priest had sat for hours right before her eyes, and he had coughed and sneezed in sound of her auditory nerves to her utter ignorance of who he was! She had stared at him, it is true, as she told her husband, and thought at the time something was very remarkable about him; and now it was all explained—he was a Catholic priest! Had she known it—had she possessed the slightest inkling, would she not have scrutinized his forehead? would she not have studied his feet? His horns and his hoofs must have been amputated, or somebody would have seen them. Mrs. Huldah continued repeating it over, "A Catholic priest in our own house, under my very eye, and I not know it! What a loss and mistake!"

Nor was Mrs. Huldah alone in her lamentations. All Sunapee would have turned out *en masse* to get a sight at this representative of the kingdom of anti-Christ.

So great had been the mortification on account of Dodds and Boggs, there was not a tithe of that bigotry and bitterness expressed as would have been the fact had those "elders" proved true and the case gone the other way.

Public opinion had indeed received a decisive check, and the simple dwellers around Kearsarge Mount and Sunapee Lake could scarcely credit their own senses. Two weeks previously every voice was crying out against Popery, insisting that no Papists should be allowed to remain in the vicinity.. Up to the day of the trial such had been the demand of the people.

Yet the sun had gone down upon a complete reversal of opinion. The "elders" had fled in ignominy, while a priest of the hated Church had braved their animosity, and, unknown, stood in their midst ready to defend his own. They were unreconciled to the result, but, perforce, must submit to the confession and humiliation.

Soon it began to be noised abroad that Mr. Ferrol was preaching from his pulpit strange doctrines. Indeed, before now the few members of his congregation had not known how to interpret him upon some occasions. That is, they now remembered thinking that he advanced some novel theories, and gave utterance to speculative ideas which were quite new to them.

As we have said, St. Mark's congregation was a small one. For twenty miles around came all the Episcopalians to St. Mark's. Some families came but once or twice a year, others once in a month. Greatly in a minority were the disciples of King Henry and Queen Elizabeth, the majority of the elect preferring to follow John Wesley or Roger Williams. Another sect, called

Congregationalists—their teachings embodied in what is termed the Plymouth platform—had a name and church in that part of Duxbury known as King's Hill. From all of these the Adventists had gathered a goodly number, leaving the original societies lamenting over sheep gone astray.

The Episcopalians had remained more faithful than the others, as, indeed, was necessary in order to maintain a body at all; and what was their reward? To be deserted by their minister?

This question came not to be asked until after the second and third visit of Father English, at the last of which it became known that Mrs. Forsyth and Ethel had been baptized Catholics.

The fact that Mr. Ferrol was so much in company of the priest, both at his own house and at "Bird'snest," tended to increase the suspicion that he was vacillating —that he was at least in great danger.

He became fully convinced—became a convert in heart to the true Church, and yet hesitated to take the final step.

But this could not last. His conscience gave him no rest, although he thought to pacify it by an enumeration of the good he could do in leading along his congregation.

In doing this he was too precipitate. Having become thoroughly grounded himself in the ancient faith, he became also full of zeal and confidence. He forgot by what gentle means he had been led along, how gradually the new light had been let in upon him, and how incalculable had been the influence of reading upon the subject for many years. Mr. Ferrol's tact was at fault; his congregation took the alarm. A petition, signed by every communicant of St. Mark's, reached the Bishop by the same mail as did Mr. Ferrol's letter of explanation and request. The petition was for the pastor's discontinuance of services, and Mr. Ferrol's announcement of a change of religious views was accompanied by a tender of his resignation.

By the earliest mail came the Bishop's curt reply—respectful, acquiescent.

Mr. Ferrol liked not to acknowledge himself disappointed; nevertheless, he was so, in a certain sense. He had expected expostulation, if not entreaties, "even as a father would entreat a son." He had thought it likely he would be summoned to the Bishop's house, that he would be catechised, reasoned with, persuaded: he was not, then, prepared for this instant, willing rending asunder of ties that had bound him to his Bishop and his church. This was painful as well as humiliating.

The Bishop, however, had some experience in these matters. Rev. James Ferrol was not his first spiritual son who had gone over to Rome; therefore the Bishop knew well how futile would be all his efforts to retain him within his fold. Time and eloquence would be wasted. He had only to let him go whither he had already gone.

This occurred just before Christmas. The Bishop's letter, coming sooner than had been anticipated, put a stay upon all proceedings which had been inaugurated to celebrate worthily the great feast-day of the Church.

They were those unusual Catholic demonstrations which had so alarmed the laity, and which had finally induced Mr. Ferrol to state his views to his Bishop, being impelled thereto by a sense of duty. As a consequence, St. Mark's was closed before Christmas Day, which day of joy and rejoicing found Mr. Ferrol, his sister and nephew, with the family at "Bird'snest"—all guests of Father English at Claremont.

It was on this Christmas Day, in the small but beautifully decorated church, before the altar, blazing with candles and perfumed with flowers and incense, that Mr. Ferrol and Mrs. Brann bowed their brows for the cleansing waters of baptism, and lifted up their souls to meet the breath of the Holy Comforter.

From this time Mr. Ferrol felt no more grief for that which was lost, but joy and thankfulness for that which he had gained. And, indeed, it was a "Merry Christmas" that, around the generous board of Father English. Even Basil was glad and happy. He had anticipated a sermon and long faces and sepulchral groans. Nothing of the kind. Francisco and Beatrice laughed heartily, as did Ethel, at the numerous tales and jests that enlivened the feast.

On the day succeeding Christmas all started for home, laden with many kind wishes and benedictions of their friend, the priest.

The Willoughbys had never known sleigh-riding in their own country. They professed very much to like it because it was polite and kind to do so, but they were, in truth, afraid and slightly sea-sick.

The return was less pleasant than their former journey. The sun became obscured, and a driving storm of snow made everything appear as in a whirl.

Their situation, at length, became quite serious, as the roads were blocked here and there with deep drifts. More than once the long, double sleigh turned upon its side, wheeling all out into the snow. No permanent damage was done, however, and the driver being skillful

and courageous, brought them all right, though late, at
"Bird'snest," where all tarried for the night.

Such a stormy Christmas as this the natives of Mexico
had never seen. To them it was very odd, as well as
was the excessive cold. They came to the resolution
that they should not go out much during the winter.
They expressed themselves as quite willing to forego all
the beauties and pleasures of which Basil and Ethel
spoke so rapturously, and leave them to enjoy the sleigh-
rides and turn-overs.

Mrs. Braun had still continued her membership with
the Congregational church where she had last lived in
New York. After her return from Claremont she wrote
at once to the pastor, stating the change she had made,
her baptism into the Catholic Church, and requesting
that her name be stricken from the list of members.

A reply did not come so soon, nor was it so brief as
was her brother's from the Bishop. It came, however,
after a few weeks, and the following is the wording of it:*

JOHNSTOWN, N. Y., July 14, 18—

At a meeting of the Congregational Church of Johnstown,
held July 9, 18—, to consider the statement of Mrs. Mary
Braun, that she has united with the Roman Catholic Church,
and her request that her name be erased from our list of
members, it was voted that the following reply be sent to
Mrs. Braun, and the same entered upon our records:

We deeply regret the step you have taken and disapprove
of your leaving us, in violation of your covenant obligation to
serve Christ with us. We wish to declare unequivocally that
it is our firm conviction that you have gone over to a church
which holds and teaches errors, and doctrines contrary to the

---

*A literal copy of a letter written to a convert by her
former Congregational pastor.

Word of God and perilous to the soul; that we cannot support nor countenance these errors, and that you have deceived yourself in embracing them and in trusting to the teachings of the Roman Catholic Church, rather than simply adhering to the pure Word of God, which He has given us as the rule of our faith and practice in all matters pertaining to our salvation.

If you are sincere and honestly follow the dictates of your conscience in the step you have taken, we claim no right to interfere with your liberty to form and hold your religious opinions, nor do we wish to persecute, or pronounce anathemas upon you. This would not be exercising the spirit of Jesus. Let God be judge. The responsibility of your action must rest with you. We cannot cease to pray that you may see your error and come and trust directly in Christ as the Saviour and Mediator whom God alone has appointed for us, and in whom alone we can find what the soul, polluted with sin and oppressed with guilt, cannot find in the observance of any church ritual, or anywhere else but in Jesus alone.

While, therefore, we disapprove the course you have taken in going out from us, we feel that the spirit of our religion demands that we count you not as an enemy, but admonish you as a friend, and to exercise towards you that love which never faileth, hoping that God may yet lead you from the bondage of human device to that simple faith in Jesus, which, above all things else, purifies the heart and fits us for heavenly peace.

Resolved, That Mrs. Mary Braun no longer be considered a member of this church, and that her name be erased from our roll of membership.

SAMUEL DANA, *Acting Pastor.*

The reader may make his own comments.

CHAPTER XX.

MR. FERROL'S SUCCESSOR—AN INHERITANCE.

IT was impossible but that, so many important personages having gone over to Rome, remarks and criticisms should follow. The fact—noised abroad through some unknown channel, though probably from disaffected members of St. Mark's—was deemed surprising, inconceivable. One thing, a memory of the past, prevented any considerable demonstrations. Both Mr. Reubens and Elder Stunner held in wholesome remembrance the ineffectual outbreak which had occurred at Claremont at the time of the establishment of the "Popish" church. They recalled how the priest had appealed to law on the part of his insulted and outraged Irish; that the offenders had suffered fines and imprisonment, and that, after all, the Church had remained upon its Rock, and no winds and waves of wrathful words had prevented its permanent growth.

True, a less upright judge and jury might be found at Sunapee and Duxbury; but on the whole it was deemed best for hostilities to be confined to verbal protestations, and multiplied prayers for the overthrow of Satan's power appearing in their midst.

Mr. Ferrol's Bishop was an exceedingly prompt person, for on that gentleman's return from Claremont he found a successor already established in the house.

The parsonage had been left in charge of the servant girl and a young friend of hers. She was surprised, but could not refuse the demand of the new incumbent to take up his abode, rude and uncivil as she deemed it.

Therefore, it happened that on arriving at St. Mark's, cold and fasting, Mr. Ferrol and his sister were received in their own house (as they had still supposed it) as strangers and guests, by a very young man, Mr. Eugene Arlington, who but one week previous had become entitled to the reverend prefix. Almost before the new converts had shaken the snow from their feet the young pastor of St. Mark's was exhibiting his credentials, taking it for granted they would throw poor Mr. Ferrol into dismay and agonies of anticipated homelessness and starvation.

"All right, Mr. Arlington," returned Mr. Ferrol, his heart sinking for the moment before the supercilious arrogance of his boy successor; "after a day. or two, soon as practicable, I will make arrangements for vacating the premises."

"Yes, yes, of course; but you can see the house is small, and there are three of you. I have had the room you occupied arranged for myself, and——"

"My room—for yourself, sir?" demanded Mr. Ferrol, rising to his feet. "How dared you have the impudence, the insolence, to invade my home during my absence, and the unparalleled audacity of making yourself master in my own room, sacred to myself, until I surrender it to you?"

"My Bishop's letters, sir—you must not forget they

install me as pastor of St. Mark's, and, of course, master of the parsonage."

"The Bishop's letters give you no authority for forgetting that you should be a gentleman."

"You appear not to be aware, sir, that by forswearing your church and going over to Rome you have forfeited——"

"Cease, if you please. Your judgment upon my course is of very little importance. Basil," turning to his nephew, "tell Jane to prepare us some supper."

Mrs. Braun, unobserved by her brother, had already gone out to give orders to Jane; the tea was therefore in rapid progress.

And now Mr. Ferrol opened his own letter from the Bishop. Reading it, he handed it to Mr. Arlington without a word. The Bishop had suggested that Mr. Ferrol entertain Mr. Arlington for a few days, say until the first of January, by which time he thought it probable Mr. Ferrol might find it convenient to vacate the parsonage.

Mr. Arlington returned the letter, somewhat crestfallen; for he, indeed, remembered the Bishop having said something to the same effect. He rallied, however, quickly:

"O, well, we may get on together for a few days; but I thought you would prefer to go at once, perhaps."

"Out in the storm—to-night—after a jaunt of thirty miles? No, I do not propose it. I shall remain here until January first. When did you arrive?"

"The night before last. We had Christmas services, though, of course, but few were present, as my coming was not expected."

Mr. Ferrol remained silent until summoned to the dining-room.

"Well, Jane, did you have a merry Christmas?" he said, after saying grace, proceeding to handle the carving-knife.

Jane answered in trembling tones, and soon after blew her nose, which told that her eyes had been full of tears and her head of sadness on account of the unusual Christmas of this strange year.

Poor Jane! She had lived six years in Mr. Ferrol's house. It had become a home to her. She had become attached to each inmate. The future was all uncertain and unknown. Mr. Arlington had spoken about retaining her, but she was not pleased with his lordly ways. Still, she would prefer to stay at the parsonage if she could not accompany the family in their approaching flitting.

Mr. Ferrol's resentment and proper assertion of dignity in parrying the insults of Mr. Arlington had an ameliorating effect upon the latter. He had got it into his head that the Anglican Church was the finest, most royal institution in the world. To be an ordained minister in its communion was a dignity next to that of its supreme earthly head—the reigning sovereign of England. In his opinion, to abdicate such a position and become a mere layman in the Church of Rome, a plebeian with common people, ruled over by a tyrannous hierarchy of Bishops, Cardinals and Pope, was an act of absurdity, if not of imbecility or insanity. Mr. Arlington had made up his mind to this, and had decided to treat Mr. Ferrol accordingly. He had premeditated all this arrogance and cruel impoliteness of which we have seen him guilty. Finding his enemy gone temporarily, he found it more easy to carry out his designs. He had fancied Mr. Ferrol to be a man with-

out a friend, save, perhaps, the poor parish priest who
had enticed him from his best good. It would be as
well to allow the recusant Episcopalian to see how low
he had fallen by early showing him what he might have
to expect in the way of obloquy and scorn. Therefore,
as we have seen, Mr. Arlington began with a high hand,
never doubting but he could carry out his role right
loftily. He was beginning to see his error by degrees;
still more when he perused his Bishop's letter to his
predecessor. The Bishop had written respectfully and
gentlemanly, in contrast to his own boarishness, and
had given him the privilege of remaining for days,
while he would have bidden him go straightway. However, Mr. Arlington's chagrin, at first slight, was
doomed to be more profound.

Soon after supper Mr. Ferrol told Jane quietly to
remove Mr. Arlington's luggage from his own to the
blue room up stairs; after seeing that this was done he
said politely to Mr. Arlington:

"Mr. Arlington, as I am very weary I will retire.
You will find the spare chamber, whither has been
removed your luggage, at your disposal. It is a room
equally as comfortable as my own, but for obvious reasons
you will see that I prefer my accustomed place. I will
bid you good night, sir," and Mr. Ferrol bowed and
withdrew.

Mr. Arlington drummed with his fingers upon the
table, and came near whistling. He realized that he
had made a simpleton of himself, and he wished the
whole thing was to be done over again. He took up a
late number of the *Eagle*, hoping, in reading, to forget
his uneasiness, when a paragraph caught his eye which
at once riveted his attention. It was like this:

"The rumor has of late been confirmed that the Rev. Mr. Ferrol, about to become a convert to Catholicism, has fallen heir to a large fortune, willed to him by his uncle, the late James Ferrol, of Sacramento, California. We tender our congratulations to the Rev. gentleman, and hope he will not forget the editor in his distribution of holiday presents."

"Oh!" sighed Mr. Arlington, throwing down the paper, and nervously pacing the floor, "this accounts for his independent bearing, and his flinging back my insults in my very teeth! I thought him a poor dog, who would not mind my thrusting him into the street; and here he proves to be a rich fellow, who would scorn longer to make his home in a place like this! What a mistake! I might have made myself on good terms with him, and hereafter been invited —who knows?—to his fine mansion, his wine cellar, his choicest habanas!" Thus the youthful clergyman went on dreaming of what might have been, occasionally awakening to the bitter memory of his unpardonable rudeness.

In the morning Mr. Ferrol was at a loss to account for the air of deference and politeness with which Mr. Arlington invariably treated him. At length Basil slyly came up to his uncle, his finger marking the item, the reading of which had caused the great change in Mr. Arlington's tactics. Mr. Ferrol read it silently, and said nothing. It occurred to him, however, that Mr. Arlington's politeness was to the heir of a fortune, and not to plain Mr. Ferrol. However, Mr. Ferrol was not unforgiving. He had only to remember his own youth and follies to fling the mantle of charity over one whom the passage of years and experience might make wiser and nobler.

Thus the few remaining days passed in harmony at the parsonage, Mr. Ferrol not appearing to remember the incidents following his return from Claremont, and Mr. Arlington, deeply grateful, as he was ashamed, learned to esteem the gentleman he had so underrated and despised. He had been taught a lesson, which would be useful to him while life should last.

And, after all, how much should be excusable in youth? In youth, which has so bitterly to mourn over her faults; and all along through life even—stumbling and falling—doing what she wishes she had not, hiding her face for shame, seeing the cynic and the scoffer not afar!

"What!" you say, "condone the faults of Mr. Arlington—his disrespect to his superior in word and deed—his relapse from contempt and sudden accumulation of respect for his Christian brother when he finds him wealthy and not in poverty—such conduct was mean and ignoble!"

Then why not learn from examples similar to this, of which many are furnished you, yourself to do differently, gentle reader?

Not alone the "world," but Christians like yourself—yea, the so-called Catholic bows the head and bends the knee to him who has plenty of money. The poor, the beloved of Christ, inheritors of the kingdom of Heaven, however good, how wise soever, may carry their cross, fainting, weary, without your helping hand, your encouraging word. Reflect if it be not so.

It must not be supposed that Mr. Ferrol gained his first knowledge of his good fortune from this item in the *Eagle*. The *Eagle* had gained its information from one of its exchanges, published in the city wherein the legal papers had been executed. For several weeks, both Mrs. Braun and her son had known of their relative's accession to wealth; though they had not proclaimed it from the housetops. There was a marked change also in the manners of various members of St. Mark's. Those even who had been most fault-finding, who had pronounced it a shame and a disgrace any longer to be ministered unto by a clergyman who thought proper devotions should be paid to the Blessed Virgin Mary, came forward with many gracious regrets for his approaching departure, and many assurances of eternal and grateful remembrance.

"It was *such* a pity," more than one said, "that just as Mr. Ferrol became wealthy, he should not only cease to be their pastor, but should have gone over to the Church of Rome." By remaining an Episcopalian he could have beautified St. Mark's, enlarged and adorned the parsonage, built a parish school, and been such a credit and ornament to them!

So, at last, it was hard for his people to give up Mr. Ferrol, so strong is the hold of money upon human admiration.

It was only through the *Eagle*, also, that the dwellers at "Bird'snest" learned the good news with regard to their friend.

The fact of his poverty, and the support of his sister and nephew, had occasioned Mrs. Forsyth considerable uneasiness, since she had known of his Catholic tendencies.

What his plans for the future might be she had no idea; with the loss of his parish, whither should he put forth his hand? A sense of delicacy had prevented her from speaking to him upon the subject.

Now she saw clearly God had provided, and, pecuniarily, it would be well with her friends.

Had Mr. Ferrol's mind and heart remained unattracted by the truths of Catholicity, and he still had been the conscientious pastor of the Episcopal church, upon this legacy from his uncle he would again have prostrated himself at the feet of Mrs. Forsyth, even at the risk of a third or fourth refusal.

Lois had been his one earthly love. She was his *beau ideal* of earthly womanhood. Unconsciously to herself, but perceptibly to him, she had influenced his character for the better, causing him to despise his vanity, to love simplicity, to become an earnest, honest worker for God and man.

However, when Mr. Ferrol was first apprised of his uncle's death and bequest (he had heard nothing of him living since a score of years), he had already resolved, by God's grace, to become a Catholic.

For the present, Mr. Ferrol took the advice of Father English, with his sister and nephew taking rooms at the "Newport House" at Claremont. He would be near church, and have access to both Father English's pleasant society and valuable library.

On the last day of the year, then, the former rector of St. Mark's bade adieu to former home and friends, parting with Mr. Arlington on extremely good terms, and leaving the faithful Jane as the latter's housekeeper.

"Birds' nest" would fain have delayed them on their journey for a day or two, instead of which they could only be detained but for a few minutes. Quite an ado was made all around.

"It would be so lonely," said Ethel.

"We cannot even expect you now, and there has been much pleasure even in expecting you," said Mrs. Forsyth.

"You may still expect me, for I am bound to come; and I'll take you girls out sleigh-riding, and carry you back with me, may be," said Basil, glancing around, but allowing his eyes to fall upon Beatrice lastly.

"Yes, you are not going so very far," said Beatrice.

"Only thirty miles—it is not across the plains, nor over the ocean," remarked Francisco.

"I think we can survive the separation," put in Ethel.

"Are you not promised to come to Claremont once in a month? that is not long; meantime take care of yourselves. Master Francisco, be a careful head of the house," was Mr. Ferrol's parting injunction.

In saying his adieu to Beatrice, Basil had managed to present her with a tiny parcel wrapped in tissue paper. Surprised at this, and wishing to make a return of favor, she caught up her prayer-book, lying upon a table, and pressed it into his hands.

"But you will wish it," pleaded Basil, though longing to retain what he would prize so much on account of the giver.

"Oh, no, I have another; read it every day, please; when you go to Mass think of me," and these were the last words of Basil and Beatrice.

Mrs. Braun was quite affected—any change was trying to her, and she was aware how much she should feel the loss of her friends at "Bird'snest."

"If you fall out in the snow, pick yourselves up, and be a good boy, Basil," was Ethel's last word, the jingling bells mingling therewith.

CHAPTER XXI.

A STRANGER AT "BIRD'SNEST" AND A REUNION.

THE cold, piercing winds and many snows of winter in due time gave place to balmy spring. This was a delightful change to the inmates of "Bird'snest," especially to those who were natives of the South. The grounds were again green and velvety, lilacs were blooming, birds were singing amid the leafy trees, and the surface of the lake was sunny and placid. Long and monotonous had been the dreary winter; so charming and welcome was the soft-footed spring.

One afternoon Ethel and her cousins were returning from a flower excursion. The day had proved much warmer than any one preceding, and the party entering the shade, Francisco took off his summer hat and with it fanned himself. The stage overtook them, and as they stepped aside to avoid the dust they partially halted, glancing up as they did so. They observed the face of a gentleman passenger light up with surprise, and the next moment he touched his hat and bowed to Francisco. The coach slowly rolled on, leaving the flower gatherers lost in conjecture as to who the stranger could be.

"Did you ever see him before?" inquired Ethel.

"Not to my knowledge; and yet—but who could recognize me, an utter stranger—he probab'y mistook me for another person," was the young man's conclusion.

"But see—the stage is stopp'ng at 'Bird'snest,'" cried Beatrice and Ethel in the same breath.

It was true. A minute later the stranger was alighting, and the young people hurried onward to give him greeting.

"Is not this the late Colonel Willoughby's son?" said the gentleman, extending a hand to Francisco.

The latter bowed, accepting the proffered cordiality.

"I have the advantage of you, I perceive. It is not strange you do not remember me; it was several years ago that I often saw you in your father's house. Is Mrs. Willoughby, your mother, at home? Let us see if she recognizes me. Please say to her a stranger would see her."

He was ushered into the parlor, still waited on by Francisco, while Ethel summoned Mrs. Willoughby.

"O, auntie, a strange gentleman wants to see you; he is waiting in the parlor; we saw him in the stage coach, and he bowed to Francisco, and he stopped here; who can he be? He was about to send in his card, but retained it, wishing to see if you would recognize him. Hurry, auntie, please—we are dying to know who he may be."

In reply to Ethel Mrs. Willoughby averred that she had not the faintest idea who the visitor could be. A sudden thought chilled her.

"Is he very, very dark?" she inquired.

"Yes; but his countenance is very pleasant; I don't think you need fear him," replied Ethel, observing her aunt's sudden terror.

"I am sure he is only a friend, mamma," spoke Beatrice, assuredly.

Tremblingly Mrs. Willoughby entered the room to meet, not her cousin Octave Geoffrion, as she had feared, but one whom she instantly recognized—Mr. Basil Braun! It was strange she had not thought of him. But his name had been for months almost unmentioned.

"I received your letter of surprising import, madam, after some delays, and as soon as practicable arranged to come on in person. You know all about what length of time is required for the long, tedious journey. I could not wait for the passage of any more slow letters; I could be satisfied only in coming. Where is this young Basil Braun of whom your letter made mention?"

"Then you do think he may be a relative of yours?"

"I had a son by that name, who would be about the age of the young person you speak of. His mother was a sister of James Ferrol. Do you imagine, then, there can be a doubt?"

"Is it possible? So many months have elapsed since the writing of the letter that we had ceased to think about it; although I have known——"

Mrs. Willoughby hesitated and the gentleman continued:

"Excuse me, madam; does Mr. Ferrol live in the vicinity?"

"When my letter to you was written, sir, he was residing where he had lived for many years, about three miles from here. At the beginning of the present year he removed temporarily to Claremont, a small town about thirty miles distant."

"And the boy is still with him?"

"He is, Mr. Braun."

"Is Mr. Ferrol a married man?"

"He has never married. He is boarding at present at a public house."

"Are you much acquainted with Mr. Ferrol?"

"We are very good friends. He has been the life-long friend of my sister-in-law, Mrs. Forsyth."

"Do you know—have you ever heard him speak of or refer to his sister, the mother of young Basil?"

Mrs. Willoughby became perplexed. She remembered Mr. Ferrol's former charge to say nothing of Mrs. Braun in the letter. But she was a lover of truth and straightforwardness. Here was Mr. Braun—why should she equivocate? If wrong had been sometime committed, let it be righted. Therefore she spoke up truly, as if suspecting nothing:

"Basil's mother, Mrs. Braun, is still residing with her brother——"

"What! Mary still living—residing with her brother?" exclaimed Mr. Braun, rising hastily and rushing across the room. "Do I hear aright? Do you say Basil's mother is still living?" cried the gentleman, striking his forehead with his clenched hand, as if to drive away this deceitful phantom of his imagination.

"Pray calm yourself, sir; I asserted the truth; Mrs. Braun is our dear friend; we saw her not one month ago."

"O, my God! and all this time I have thought her dead! I was solemnly assured that she had died, and our child also. O, great heavens! how have I been sinned against, how greatly have I suffered!"

"She, too, has suffered," remarked the lady, unwilling that Mr. Braun should consider himself the only person aggrieved.

"How could it all have happened? how was it possible? But it all came through her, the curse of my life. Ah! I begin to see it now. She was my wife's friend; she professed to have been with her on her death-bed; she brought me what was purported to be her dying farewell; she brought me the jewels I had given her—given Mary, my beloved wife. I wept bitter tears for my dead wife, and *she* wept with me—that friend who professed to have been with Mary on her death-bed! She was mistress of the arts; she wove her snares finely. I was caught in her meshes—I was a doomed man!"

Mr. Braun had been speaking as if to himself. Partially recovering, he apologized:

"Your pardon, my lady. Have indulgence for these incoherencies: I am almost mad with the suddenness of this knowledge of how we were both betrayed—my Mary and I. Caroline was afterwards, as I thought, my lawful wife, but never like Mary, the wife of my heart. Mary dead—as I believed—reigned there supreme. You will remember, Mrs. Willoughby, the disgraceful death of Mary's rival at Santa Fé. Little did I dream what deadly cause I had for loathing her!"

The man bowed his head in his hands, and shook with emotion. Silence prevailed. At length he raised his head and threw back the hair from his brow, demanding impetuously:

"And did Mary believe me faithless? What did she, what could she believe through all these years? Surely I dream—I have had dreams like this before—that she was living and I was to meet her—but I awoke, and why do I not now awake?"

Francisco instinctively feared delirium, and, taking

the man's hand, led him out upon the veranda. Seating him, he placed his cool palm upon the stranger's brow, remarking soothingly:

"You must be quiet now and calm. Think how happy Mrs. Braun and Basil will be to see you. You have a fine noble boy, and he has a lovely mother."

"And I have so long been deprived of them!" moaned the stranger, disconsolately.

"Please do not think of that, but of your happiness in having them restored to you."

By degrees the gentleman became quiet and talked more rationally, when Mrs. Forsyth and the other members of the household came also out to entertain him. Soon came the summons for tea, which all obeyed with alacrity.

Great attention was given to Mr. Braun to enable him to retain his comparative tranquillity, and, as he had been faint from fasting and weariness, he had already become quite refreshed with the good cheer and the bountiful repast, when, through the open door, came the sound of merry voices, and then hasty footsteps, followed by young Basil's joyous voice

"Here we all are, hungry as bears—just in good time. Thought we would take you by surprise this once—we wanted to see you so bad——"

Mr. Ferrol stopped short in the midst of his speech, and his sister, who brought up the rear, without noticing that a stranger was present, saluted her friends, whom she thought were unusually subdued and undemonstrative, when suddenly the eyes of Mr. Braun met her own. He had arisen from his seat, and was just in time to catch her in his arms as she was reeling to the floor. What followed can better be imagined than described.

Until after Mr. Braun had made a thorough explanation, Mr. Ferrol maintained an indignant and injured air; but after all had been brought to light, and even Mary, the injured wife, saw how all the fault rested on the girl friend of her youth, Mr. Ferrol extended the hand of hearty forgiveness and welcome to his restored brother-in-law.

"A singular coincidence that we should have happened over to-day. It was Basil's plan and his mother's. They thought they wanted to see you all, while I was greatly anxious to see the old place in its spring garb," said Mr. Ferrol.

"So you did not wish to see us—how unkind of you," returned Ethel.

As we have said, both Mr. Ferrol and his sister were satisfied with Mr. Braun's rehearsal of the great wrong which had been wrought for himself and family. They saw clearly that he was guiltless in the matter, that he had been sinned against and had suffered, as well themselves.

Frank Houghton and his sister Caroline had lived near neighbors to Mr. and Mrs. Braun from the time of the latters' marriage. An intimate friendship had long existed between the two ladies, though Mr. Braun and Frank had been simply on friendly terms. For some reason young Houghton became dissatisfied, sold the homestead he had inherited, and took his departure, as he himself said, for a long tramp. Before leaving he had divided his substance with his sister, and had seen her comfortably established in the family of Mr. Braun.

Caroline Houghton had also been the friend of Mary Ferrol before the latter became Mrs. Braun. That there should be a strong attachment between the two was rather surprising, since they could not have been more unlike. Mary was quiet, gentle, thoughtful, affectionate; she was lady-like, truthful, womanly. Caroline was the reverse in all these qualities. She could be, however, whatever she chose for the occasion—whatever was most expedient. Duplicity was her leading characteristic. With a strong will-power, she could fascinate with her scintillant yet determined eye, and command obedience with her haughty tone and dominant manner.

With her arts she completely beguiled poor, guileless, artless Mary Ferrol. She knew how to do this by instinct as well as by study and practice; and she plied flattery so delicately, yet so strongly, that Mary, her victim, was fooled as was the simple fly by the wicked spider in the story.

As Mary was trusting and loving, Caroline liked to exercise over her an authority, which she feigned was that of careful, earnest affection. For hours Mary would sit at the feet of Caroline, listening to the latter's rhapsodies over people and things, her sarcasms, her witticisms, which had forever for their winding up something like this:

"You know, Mary dear, there is but one person in the world who just suits me in every way, and that one is you, Mary."

"I am not brilliant, like you, Caroline. We are not alike—why do you like me? I often wonder why," Mary would reply.

"Because I must love some one, I suppose, and you are that only 'some one' in all the world. Nobody else cares for me but you."

And this, perhaps, was the true reason why Mary,

despite some intuitions, still clung to Caroline—because no one else was really her friend.

"Everybody else breaks with me," Caroline would say. "They become offended by what I cannot help saying; they show weak, shallow natures; but you, Mary, are true at heart, and do not fly up and off at a careless word. I love you so much for that; I depend on you always to be my friend."

And so Mary, admiring depth and constancy in friendship, would renew her resolves of keeping true. Believing Caroline sincere—that Caroline who would turn away murmuring, "Simple little goose."

It was but a short time before the birth of Basil that Caroline took up her abode with the Brauns. Whether it was before this entrance into the family that she conceived the project she afterwards carried out may not be known. We may give her the benefit of the doubt, and not suspect her of thus early cherishing her later deadly designs.

About a year after Frank Houghton's departure for the South he wrote a letter to Mr. Braun, giving glowing accounts of the Mexican country, and the remarkable facilities for money-making which it presented.

Mr. Braun at once conceived the idea of going unto the distant field for gain and speculation. He could see no prospect ahead in this little town of acquiring more than a competence, if hardly that, by toil and slow degrees. He, therefore, bade wife and child a long adieu —alas! so much longer than he had counted upon. Caroline was left with Mary, and it had been hoped all would go well.

One year, two years passed, and frequent letters were received by Mary from her husband and by Caroline from her brother.

Frank at length began to write in glowing terms of the success Mr. Braun was meeting. In one letter he said: "Mr. Braun is making money hand over hand. He will become a millionaire if he keeps on. I do not understand it. I wish I had his head; but I am as poor as the patient man's turkey, and fear I always shall be. Cal, why didn't you be smart enough and marry this Braun, instead of giving him up to that milk-and-water wife of his, for whom he is going to send one of these days? I tell you what, she will live like a princess. What a pity it is not you who are his wife! By the way, is Mrs. Braun in good health?"

Caroline, who had allowed Mrs. Braun to read Frank's former letters, kept this one concealed until, reading it over day after day, she had this part of it by heart, then she threw the letter into the fire.

Did Frank Houghton *intend* to give a hint? Knowing his sister well, did he suppose anything further was necessary for leading her to a course of action which he wished her to pursue, and to which she at once applied herself?

Caroline had been in the habit of bringing letters to and from the postoffice. An easy matter was it, then, for her to appropriate Basil Braun's letters, and never give them to his wife. Just as easy to destroy Mrs. Braun's letters to her husband, which never went so far as the postoffice. She wrote to Frank that the child Basil had died, and that his mother, worn out with watching, anxiety and grief, was upon a bed of sickness. After the lapse of a few weeks she again wrote to Mr. Braun, as if at the dictation of his wife, expressing great grief for the child, and utter disinclination to live longer in a world which had nothing desirable to offer, etc., etc.

This letter she enclosed in one to her brother, charging him to retain the same until he should receive a second missive, when, with an apology of forgetfulness, he might deliver both at once.

His second letter was written a month later, stating the particulars of Mrs. Braun's sickness and death, tender messages of dying love, and so forth. Also, she stated to Mr. Braun that he need have no misgivings or anxiety: she had done and had required to be done for poor Mary, living and dead, all that he could have done had he been present. That, as now poor Mary was gone and there was nothing to keep her, she should start, as soon as she recovered from her fatigue, to join her brother, and she would bring to him some keepsakes which poor Mary had wished to be placed into his own hands.

Caroline never flinched from carrying out this dastardly programme. She saw poor Mary anxious, tearful, hopeless, at the absence of letters. She had the cruelty to express for her the deepest sympathy, while at the same moment insinuating that he may have found one whom he loved more. Nay, she showed her a letter from Frank not simply intimating, but asserting, that a rich Spaniard's daughter might prove a too formidable rival to his wife. Caroline even prided herself upon her humanity. Others less conscientious, she reasoned, would have poisoned both Mary and the child. I spare them. I leave them life after I have rendered it worthless to them.

Mary went to her brother, without knowing the intention of Caroline to go down to New Mexico. The latter had spoken of visiting some distant relatives in an opposite direction. She had parted from Mary (helping her off most efficiently) with every demonstration of affection, promising to write at an early day, and to come and make her a long visit after a few weeks.

And Mary Braun had never seen or heard of Caroline Houghton again. The false, wicked woman thoroughly perfected her schemes and found herself the wife of Basil Braun. Only *she* knew she was not his wife. But she was in a land where were no railroads, no telegraphic wires; where communication with the States was slow and uncertain; where she might not see in a life-time an old familiar face. She had no fear that her treachery and sin would be discovered. But the anticipated happiness never satisfied her selfish, scheming nature. With plenty of wealth at her command, she sought only sensual enjoyments. Drinking wine to excess, she sunk lower and more low, till, her womanhood lost, she came to the shameful death, as narrated by Mrs. Willoughby to Mrs. Forsyth—death in a drunken quarrel with some Mexican women.

CHAPTER XXII.

A NEW PROJECT—CONSIDERABLE CONSULTATION.

THE young son of Basil Braun had been stunned, as it were, by the passing of these events and by this revelation. He had been under the impression that his mother was a widow. In fact, he had been told the same by the only parent he had ever known; for to Mary Braun the husband of her love was indeed dead and buried. Comparatively comforting would have been tears wept over his grave.

To find himself, then, after all these years, face to face with a stranger whom he was to call father was a novel situation. His mother, then, no longer belonged to him alone. There was a stronger arm for her to lean upon. Was he glad or sorry?

After a variety of conflicting emotions—after he had heard himself addressed as " my dear son," and received the embraces of a new-found father, he passed out silently from the bustle and confusion, the repeated exclamations and congratulations, and, going over to the lake, paced silently up and down the shore.

Was he glad or sorry? he again questioned. From early boyhood he had looked forward to becoming the support and protector of his mother. So far as possible he would be all in all to her. He had planned to carve out for himself a name and fortune all for that dear mother's sake. This demand, which he foresaw the future had for him, had been a strong element in the formation of a character, which at eighteen promised all that was manly and noble. Unconsciously, this expectation of future work and this present constant attendance upon his mother had been a support to the boy, a stimulus to endeavor, a goal for ambition.

The position had become in a moment changed. The proud boy felt weak and bewildered, as if he had fallen from a height. His dear mother belonged to another who had a prior, if not dearer, right.

Was he glad or sorry? he inquired of himself for the third time.

His mother's best good was the highest wish of his heart. His father was wealthy—she would be beyond anxiety or want; and neither she nor himself would now be dependent on his uncle during his intended college course. There was in this a satisfaction. And his father would probably take his mother with him back to the sunny clime, whose balmy breezes would fan her back to health; and for himself, should not he, too, accompany his parents to the land whither Beatrice was soon to depart? A gleam of pleasure shot from his fine eye, and an emotion which was not of sorrow swelled in his heart.

At this moment appeared Beatrice, approaching. Basil met her half-way, grasping warmly her little hand.

"I congratulate you, my friend. You have found a noble father. And now your dear mother will regain her health," said Beatrice.

"I trust so; but at first my only thought was, 'I have lost my mother.'"

"O! Basil, that would be wrong and selfish."

"Yes, I see it at length—it is all for the best. I can now say I am truly glad."

"And we are all going together back home!"

"What?"

"We are going to have you all for company during the long, tiresome journey over the plains; will not that be delightful?"

"Is it truly so?"

"Your father says he must return soon; and mamma was only waiting until some escort should be found, far or near; I am so glad you can go with us; I shall not half so much dread the journey."

"But you have Francisco all the same."

"Yes—O yes—I have dear Francisco, but I have learned to like you as a brother, too."

"I am glad to hear you say that. You are very kind. I have neither brother nor sister, and just a moment ago I felt as if I had no longer a mother. But if you will be my sister, Beatrice, I shall be quite happy."

"You ought to be very happy indeed. You have now more than I—you have a dear father."

"He shall be your father, too," returned Basil, entirely willing to share with his little "sister" this acquisition, whose desirability he so lately questioned.

"How long a time will the journey require?"

"O! weeks and weeks; you will become sick and tired of it before it ends."

"Not at all; I shall enjoy it."

"You can hunt and fish by the way."

"That will be splendid."

"And we *may* have to turn in and cook our suppers. We shall have to travel all night, jolting and shaking, for in some parts there are rocky mountains, and then we suffer with cold."

"You cannot scare me—I shall enjoy it all," said Basil, confidently, buoyant and joyous with the prospect of Beatrice for a companion.

"But there is one thing you will not be so gay over—that is, the robbers of the coaches."

"Ah, the robbers! That is what I have read about. That will be romantic; yes, I shall particularly enjoy that."

Beatrice looked at him with surprise, thinking how different were boys and girls.

"That comes from being a boy," she said, audibly.

"Of course. They are only men who attack you. Why not be a man, and give them as good as they send?"

"It is splendid to be so brave. I believe Francisco is not quite so brave as yourself, though he is a hero compared to mamma and me. We are perfect cowards."

"Did you see anything of these banditti when you came out?"

"No, not really; but we were dreadfully frightened many times. Our coaches had guards—mounted men, well armed."

"When are we going? I wish we might start to-day."

"They may have it all arranged by this time. Let us return to the house. I started out in search of you when I heard your father say to Mrs. Braun, 'I shall take you and Basil with me down to the beautiful Valley of the Rio Grandé, where you will recover bloom and health.' Then I said to mamma, 'Shall we not go with them?' to which she answered affirmatively."

"Lucky we came over yesterday."

"A special Providence, Basil; though, of course, Mr.

Braun would have lost no time in going there; but, he was so tired, and, too, it is best as it is. I am so happy it all happened here, just as it should be. What a good story this will be to tell to dear Sister Catherine! A true story of real life, and the proof will be, I shall take you to see her!"

"To see Sister Catherine? What care I for any sister but my own sister, Beatrice?"

"Ah! Sister Catherine is everybody's sister, which I am not. She is an angel on earth, which I am not. She is a saint, like the holy ones we read of."

"I shall be much more afraid of her than of the robbers. Before her I should tremble."

Again Beatrice looked at Basil with surprise. There was more than one variety of courage, evidently. She none the less strenuously determined to bring him to the test.

Basil and Beatrice had now reached the house, from the veranda of which Mr. Ferrol called out:

"So, my boy, Basil, is frightened at last. A rich father is not what the majority of boys would run away from."

"Basil and I will take our time for becoming acquainted. We will have many a gallop together over the plains," remarked Mr. Braun, glancing kindly at his son, who took the seat proffered by his uncle.

The conversation turned upon the salient features of the far country, in which Mr. Braun naturally became chief speaker. All parties admired his dignified manner, pleasant voice, fine descriptive powers; they were so charmed with all he said and acted, that it had become quite late ere Mrs. Forsyth proposed retirement for the night.

Ethel was brushing out her golden curls, while Beatrice had disrobed and said her prayers.

"You appear in great haste to close your eyes in sleep without making a single comment on all the wonderful surprises that have occurred this afternoon," said Ethel, at length.

"I am all ready, now, dear Ethel. It was so marvelous as to be almost incomprehensible. It seems now like a dream," said Beatrice.

"I suppose you arranged with Basil all about the journey. I really envy you that journey."

"Do you really? I rather dread it, though not nearly so much now, since we are to have the good company of the Brauns."

"I have been wondering why you do not invite mamma and I to accompany you. I tell you, cousin Beatrice, I shall die of loneliness after you all are gone!"

"Dear cousin Ethel, I had not thought of you being able to go. The time has been so brief, of course we have thought of almost nothing as yet. I am sure mamma will think of that; and she will insist for auntie and you to go down and spend years with us. O! what a happy thought. You must go, indeed."

"I fear mamma would object. She could not carry 'Bird'snest,' and, without 'Bird'snest,' she would be disconsolate. But, I wish you to urge the matter, Beatrice. Interest your mamma and Francisco in the project; I shall tackle Mr. Ferrol to-morrow, and get him in the notion of going. What is the use of spending one's days in this dull part of the world? I never knew how dull and dark it is till since you have been here. You and Francisco have illuminated it. When your light shall be withdrawn, what darkness!"

"And yet it is so beautiful here!"

"But imagine, if you can, how insufferable it would be to dwell here all alone with your mamma! I endured it heretofore, because I knew no difference; besides, we had Mr. Ferrol, and Mrs. Braun, and Basil. With them gone, and you gone, what is left? No, I should become a maniac!"

"Not so bad as that, I hope!"

"Another thing: What is the use to have become a Catholic, and live thirty miles away from church? Dwelling in midst of hordes of heretics, who look upon you as lunatics, and make you subjects of long prayers, that you may be enlightened and see the truth as John Wesley saw it, or as Elder Stunner and Mr. Reubens see it?"

"Poor Ethel, you shall never stay here. I am sure I cannot go and leave you; I should be very unhappy. It would distress me to live away from the church, and from the dear Sisters. Only a camp-meeting, and a Fourth of July, and a thanksgiving the year round!"

"Isn't it dismal? Would I not be in a slough of despond, and with another governess, who is to appear as you disappear? I know I should have scarlet fever and typhoid, diphtheria and pneumonia, and, at last, consumption or brain fever would end all my woes," moaned Ethel, bent upon arousing her cousin's sympathy and powerful intervention in her behalf.

"Well, you must pray, Ethel. You haven't said your prayers yet; you must pray with more faith than ever before; I am confident a way will be provided. But, let me tell you, Ethel, when you pray, be careful; always say from your inmost heart, 'not my will, but Thine be done.'"

"If only I had your faith, and your goodness, my dear, I might have hope that my prayers would be answered."

"You *must* have faith, or your prayers are vain. Say with St. Thomas, 'I believe: help Thou mine unbelief!'"

Then the angel of sleep weighed down the eyelids of the maidens, and the spirit of restful silence brooded over "Bird'snest."

Fair "Bird'snest" by the lake.

Thus slept Eden beneath the gracious smile of the Infinite, while the serpent lay coiled without.

CHAPTER XXIII.

FAIR "BIRD'SNEST" BY THE LAKE—HATRED AND REVENGE.

AT the time Ethel and Beatrice had been conversing, they had been thought to be asleep by their respective parents; both Mrs. Willoughby and Mrs. Forsyth had been discussing the same subject: that of a removal to Mexico.

As Ethel had predicted, "Bird'snest" lay in the way. What could be done with "Bird'snest?" If the cottage could be transported like the holy house of Loretto, then the question were easily answered. Could Mrs. Forsyth sell "Bird'snest?" It was the one apple of her eye—Ethel being the other. And who was there to buy it, or who had any money to pay a tithe of its value?

And the idea of "Bird'snest" belonging to another! The sacred home of her father and mother; the dear home of her few wedded years; the only home she had ever known!

"But you will be all alone with the sad memories of the past; time will pass gloomily with yourself and your child; for Ethel's sake, if not for your own, consider! Except for your own good I would not urge you; one thing should influence you to a certain

extent, however—the religious advantages you would
have with us. You need not sell 'Bird'snest;' leave it
in care of Rachel. The question is being agitated of a
railroad through from Topeka to Santa Fé. The building of this road is but a question of time. Your return
may be one of comparative ease," this said Mrs.
Willoughby.

Mrs. Forsyth replied with many arguments *pro* and
con, finally finishing with:

"Well, we will leave it now. There is no necessity
for an immediate decision. Mr. Braun can be detained
for a week, I think. You will all hold a conclave, discussing the matter. For my part, I feel at present
incapable of even a favorable leaning to your proposition; but we will leave it all now, trusting in a kind
Providence as our guide."

As we have before said, "kind Nature's sweet
restorer" embraced the inmates of the cottage by
the lake.

This sleep was soon disturbed.

Mr. Ferrel's voice resounded through the house, and
"Fire—Fire!" was his fearful word.

Simultaneously with this cry, Mr. Braun had been
awakened with a conviction that some one was in his
room. A gleam of light shot in from without, reveal-
ing the figure of a man, who appeared fumbling at the
bureau. It was but the work of a moment for this
dweller upon the plains to draw his revolver from
beneath his pillow and aim at the intruder. An oath
and a heavy fall followed.

All was wildest excitement.

Mr. Ferrol did not lose his self-possession. His aim
was to see that every life should be saved. There was

not a moment to lose, for the house had been fired in several places, and in a brief time was but one mass of flame.

The inmates had but time to catch the clothing laid off a few hours previously, with a few exceptions. Mrs. Forsyth swept her clothes-press of nearly all its contents, and, in passing, tore down from the wall the picture of Paul, her husband. Francisco and Basil bore out trunk after trunk, and Rachel saved the silver; comparatively little, however, of the contents of the house was saved. Books, pictures, precious things were reduced to ashes. Mr. Braun bore out the fainting figure of his wife, and then returned more than once to save what he could. He afterward remembered stumbling against the fallen body in his room, which at the time he had resolved to return and drag out. This the fury of the flames prevented.

Neighbors soon rushed to the scene of the fire.

Mr. Smalley, the one who lived nearest, came greatly excited. To the crowd, he said:

"I believe that fellow set the house afire. I seed him little afore dark sneaking through the bushes. I was hunting for the cows. I knew him at once—it was he. I thought he was after mischief."

"Who? Whom do you mean, neighbor Smalley? *He* is a common name hereabouts," cried several voices at once.

"Why that bogus Methodis' Elder—that State-prison scamp that 'cused these yer young folks of upsettin' himself and his hosses into the road—that's the *he* I mean."

At these words Mr. Ferrol started up; so also did Mr. Braun. The latter, however, remained silent until

Mr. Smalley had been sharply cross-questioned by Mr. Ferrol, who exclaimed:

"Where can this fellow be now? He must be in the vicinity; the whole country must be scoured."

"Aye—aye," answered one and another, expressing their readiness to be led in pursuit.

"Let us wait a little," said Mr. Braun. "I have reason to believe the villain who fired the house is very near us; that he is roasting in the fire of his own kindling."

Cries of rejoicing rent the air.

"Peace—be quiet! this is no time for cheers, when calamity has befallen our friend and neighbor. We will hear Mr. Braun's reasons for his belief," said Mr. Ferrol, with dignity.

Then Mr. Braun stated what our readers already know, which recital convinced all that robbery for his own benefit was the evil man's design, as well as arson through hatred and revenge.

As soon as the raging fire had subsided sufficiently the eager men, who had gathered in still greater numbers, demanded the precise spot to be indicated where the wretch must have fallen. This was done, and the fate of the unhappy man proved certain as their poles stirred among the embers.

Whether he had been killed outright, or disabled only, and thus left to torture, can never be known. Certain it is that the wretched man fell into his own snares, and was smitten with the sudden death he had devised for others. He had doubtless supposed the house, as usual, to be guarded only by women and boys, and had not prepared himself for the ready action of brave men.

Hospitalities without number were offered to the houseless people of "Bird'snest." These were accepted in the same spirit as proffered, and comparative calm followed the night's exciting events.

It had been difficult to persuade the owner of "Bird'snest" to leave even the coals and ashes of her home. Her heart was riven with a sense of the desolation. The loss was not deepest as a pecuniary one; but the loves and associations of a life time had been temporarily embodied only to be permanently slain. With the going out of her precious things into ashes went her soul through the fires of a purgatory. Like a statue she set apart, her face pallid, her eyes fixed upon the splendor of the hastening ruins, her cold hands clasped convulsively. Ethel knelt at her feet.

"Dear mamma, let us not mind it: you have me and I have you."

Still the mother's eyes wavered not. The death-hour of her father, the last agony of her beloved Paul, came up in review before her, torturing her afresh. Mrs. Willoughby stood by her side, and drew the fragile form close to her bosom, pressing the cold, locked hands, whispering words intended to cheer and comfort; in vain. Then Beatrice, full of faith and submission, rising up from Ethel's side, whispered:

"This is a cruel scene in your beautiful garden; but think, dear auntie, of another scene in another garden, where He sweat great drops of agony; offer this sorrow of thine to His Divine Heart, and He who has suffered will comfort thee."

The form of Beatrice had shut out the lessening flames. Her softly spoken words, as if endued with spirit and with life, awoke the woman from her partial

trance. Their meaning fell upon her sense. The
agony of Gethsemane! How often had she read it with
tearful eyes. In a moment her eyes filled with tears,
her whole countenance changed. She clasped Beatrice
in her arms, whispering:

"Angel-child, thou hast well spoken. All that I have
of grief or regret shall be offered up to Him from this
hour."

A relief came to all with these words. Francisco and
Basil, who had been standing by fearing, listening, but
not speaking, now withdrew to join the gathering of
men, who were just then in the earnest conversation
about the burglar and incendiary which has been before
recorded.

Sunapee Mount and Duxbury became tossed upon a
high sensational wave. Mr. Hartford had a new theme
for his *Eagle*, which promised to prove as lucrative as
the "outrage" of the previous season. The reappear-
ance, the crime, the horrible death of the ex-convict,
who had figured so conspicuously in the former affair,
furnished ample subject for conversation.

Not alone had Mr. Smalley recognized the man
Dodds; others had met him—one in a neighboring
town, another more near. Captain Mowbray had also
passed him by, wondering at the time at his surly
silence and apparent unrecognition. Without doubt he
had returned for one express purpose, accomplishing
more than he had intended.

Mr. and Mrs. Jonathan Towne offered their house in
hospitality to Mrs. Forsyth and her friends. Mr.
Eugene Arlington expressed great sympathy, and
offered the parsonage, so far as it would accommodate.
Mr. Billings and Mrs. Lemantha, his wife, drove over to

the one hotel, where several of the homeless were domiciled, and paid their respects. Dr. Buncombe and his strong-minded wife, arm-in-arm, came to express their commiserations and to gain some more certain information with regard to the catastrophe. The Baptist minister and the Adventist, and many more, in fact, who had never presumed to cross the threshold of "Bird's-nest," as if they had been old friends of Mrs. Forsyth, came, tendering sympathy and friendly interest.

Was it from real good nature, or from an o'ermastering curiosity? Did they not feel that with the destruction of "Bird'snest" (what they had been pleased to term) the pride of the Walsingham and the pride of the Forsyths had been brought low? That the quiet little woman in black, who had held herself so aloof, now without a house, and they knew not what means, might be a little more sociable, less reserved, and less fastidious?

Be this as it may, all were received politely.

There were those who said secretly, and others who openly professed to believe, that the calamity of fire had befallen the proprietor of "Bird'snest" because she had harbored Papists, and, likely as not, had become a Papist herself.

In olden times did not God rain fire upon Sodom and Gomorrah, and why not upon this cottage by the lake?

To one who dared suggest such an idea, Mrs. Huldah Towne flew with the ferocity of a tigress.

"You talk about those people being Papists! Does that make them any worse, I'd like to know? In my opinion, it may be that which makes them better. Were you a Papist that your child died? Were you a Papist that your heifer was struck by lightning, and that your cellar caved in, and that your garden was eaten up by grasshoppers? Papists! I'm sick of the word!"

"But I'm not the only one; most o' folks say the same thing," ventured the visitor.

"Then the most o' folks are fools!" indignantly retorted Mrs. Huldah, and she went on fearlessly: "Has nobody's home catched fire and burnt afore now? Suppose my house was to be a smoulderin' heap by to-morrow mornin', or your house, or neighbor Craft's, what would you say then? Don't talk to me! I thought you had more sense!"

Mrs. Huldah looked at her visitor with annihilating eyes.

Her visitor, however, after wavering a little, took courage and commenced, twisting her bonnet strings:

"They do say, Mrs. Towne, that you and your husband——well——that you——"

"Out with it! What is it they say?" demanded imperatively the fiery woman.

"They say"—keeping her eyes steadfastly upon Mrs. Huldah, as if to guard from any spring—"they do say that you are infidels, that you don't believe in any religion, that you have Tom Paine's book locked up in your desk, that you are worse than the heathen, almost as bad as the Papists!"

The visitor had taken advantage of Huldah's sudden state of quietude to say all she wished.

"They do, do they? and who are *they?*" demanded Mrs. Huldah, much more gently than had been put her former imperative questions.

"Why, everybody!"

"And who is everybody, pray?"

"You know as well as I. It is of no use to mention names."

"Well, you shall mention names—answer me!"

The visitor still hesitated—Mrs. Huldah still insisted.

In the confusion of the moment the visitor could recall the name of only one person whom she had ever heard affirm such a thing to be true, and, unthoughtful of the consequences, she out with it·

"Mr. Dodds said so."

She saw in a moment her mistake.

"A beautiful authority, truly! That burglar, that incendiary, that murderer in his heart is 'they!' is 'everybody!' The 'theys' and the 'everbodys' are usually just such scape-goats and villains. You have cut your own fingers. I see you are ashamed enough. I advise you to talk no more about Papists or infidels until you shall know what you are talking about. Good day."

Mrs. Huldah said these last words somewhat gently to the woman as she withdrew, ready to weep with mortification.

Left alone, Mrs. Huldah continued talking to herself, energetically drawing her waxed thread through the button-hole of a vest she was about completing:

"They may say what they please, Sunapee Mount is running down hill fast. Mr. Ferrol was a nice man, and a credit to these parts, and he is gone. To be sure he belonged to the edge of Duxbury, but it's all the same. His sister was a perfect lady, and she is gone. What a mystery about that husband of hers! A dozen years gone, and thought to be dead, and here he turns up, rich, they say; and that son of hers, a fine boy who always minded his own business, and he is gone! And all 'Bird'snest' gone—house, folks and all! Well, Sunapee Mount has had her front teeth knocked out, no mistake. She hasn't a grandeur left but her lake and her mountain, and not one big-bug to admire them. Umph! Papists! not one in a hundred knows the meaning of the word. They have been told it is something awful, something next to Satan, so they think it must be so. They have had a chance to know better since these live Papists have been in town."

Here entered her husband.

"What, alone? I thought I heard you talking to some one," he observed.

"Thinking aloud, that's all."

"Have you heard the news?"

"I heard that we—you and I—are almost as bad as Catholics—that we are infidels."

"You did? That is no news. Dodds circulated that story. He was mad because you would not consent for him to make his home with us."

"Now don't you see I was right? You was for letting him come. Wouldn't it have sounded pretty to be told all over the county that that villain had had a room beneath our roof? Jonathan, you may always know I am right. I will not work my fingers to the bone cooking and cleaning up for any man or woman that don't belong to me."

"Say, did you hear the bank had failed, and Mrs. Forsyth has lost every cent she has in the world?"

Mrs. Huldah dropped her work and stared at her husband. The old saying "misery likes company" was exemplified in her first exclamation:

"Now she will have to go to work like the rest of us!"

"She has plenty of rich relations; unlucky, wasn't it,

that her insurance policy had just run out? She hasn't a cent she can call her own

"Not even her insurance? You astonish me, Jonathan!"

"She is going with the others down South. I wouldn't wonder if she marries Ferrol after all. *He* has got the money now, and we know, Huldah, that he is not stingy with it. He would throw every dollar at her feet if she were only to say yes."

"How some people are born to good luck! Of course she will marry Mr. Ferrol."

And Jonathan Towne now set it down as a fixed certainty, because his wise wife had said so.

CHAPTER XXIV.

AT LAST—DISENTHRALLED.

ONLY a day or two remained Mrs. Forsyth and her friends at the public house at Sunapee Mount. That time was sufficient for the arrival of the tidings of the bank failure (to which Mr. Towne had alluded in his conversation with his wife), and Mrs. Forsyth was doomed to experience the truth of "misfortunes never come singly."

This second loss, however, affected not Lois Forsyth as had the first, for obvious reasons, even though she saw that by it she and her daughter were reduced to poverty. She had heeded that heaven-inspired whisper of Beatrice, and from that time her composure and spirit of submission could not be disturbed. She had at once decided to comply with Mrs. Willoughby's urgent proposal, and accompany her to her home in the South. She could not forget how, a few hours prior to the fire, she had said, "We will let Providence open the way." She could not doubt now but the way was open.

Ethel and Beatrice were conversing after the morning meal upon the one subject which was now engrossing their thoughts.

"I am so frightened, Beatrice," exclaimed Ethel.

"You should have recovered from your fright ere now," rejoined the other.

"You mistake; so I have; it is of something else I fear—my wickedness!"

"I do not understand what you mean!"

"No; well, do you not know that I am rejoicing over this burning of 'Bird'snest?'"

"Rejoicing?"

"I may as well give it the right name. Mamma would never have gone to your home if 'Bird'snest' had not burned. I am rejoicing that we are going with you. Am I not then rejoicing at the destruction of dear old 'Bird'snest?' Say, Francisco, am I not?" as that young gentleman, accompanied by Basil, entered the little private parlor, one corner of which the girls were occupying.

Explaining herself again to her boy-cousin, she asked:

"Is it a sin to be glad 'Bird'snest' is out of the way, so that mamma and I may take this much-desired journey? I am so glad that I am conscience-stricken. I feel almost as if I had myself set fire to 'Bird'snest.'"

"Perhaps you did," spoke Basil. "After all, you may be the real culprit. Perhaps the burglar was only after stealing. By the way they are burying that man's bones this morning."

"Don't tell us about it," exclaimed Ethel, covering her eyes.

"If you do nothing worse than to rejoice that you are going down with us, your penance need not be a severe one," remarked Francisco.

"But if 'Bird'snest' had not burned, I should not now be rejoicing."

Basil said:

"I have heard of people dancing on a grave."

"That is just my own feeling—that I am dancing on a grave."

"Your best way is to speedily divest yourself of any such feeling," said Francisco.

"And how?" inquired his cousin.

"Have you realized that you are really about to visit the country we have told you about—that you will see our Church of St. Francis, and St. Miguel, Our Lady of Guadalupe, and Our Lady of the Rosary? That you will see our dear Father Fiélon and our venerable Archbishop? Have we told you about his famous garden?"

"No, not one word. I suppose it is a garden of Eden —the real Garden of Eden, remodeled."

"Sacrilegious girl!"

"Where does the sacrilege come in? Which garden suffers? But no matter; tell me about it; I will not be frivolous."

Francisco remaining silent, Beatrice said:

"It is the loveliest spot in all the world. In the centre is a large fish pond, in which sport every variety of fish. In various parts are cool fountains, dashing spray continually. Every genus and species of flower are there, bedewed with drops sparkling in the sunshine. All kinds of fruit, especially every variety of grape, are here cultivated to perfection. All this you will see."

"Wicked girl that you are, dancing over a grave!"

"Wicked boy, Basil, when I was already forgetting all about it!" said Ethel, reproachfully.

"Come," said this object of reproach, "let us go take our last sail on Sunapee Lake."

"Oh! no, it would be too sad, knowing it to be the last, the very last, forever and ever," said Ethel.

However, they took a stroll out towards the ruins of the home in which all had known so much happiness, and really *did* take a last boat-ride on the lake.

On their return from this to the hotel for dinner, they were met with the news just brought by the morning's mail of the failure of the bank, in which was invested all the worldly wealth of Ethel and her mother.

A cloud came over Ethel's face; but, when she saw her mother undisturbed, she uttered no complaint.

What knew she or her mother of the evils of poverty? Neither of them, in the least, realized as yet the state to which they had been reduced in the last half-day.

"How do you suppose the bank came to fail the same day that our home was burned?" inquired Ethel of Mr. Ferrol.

"It was a striking coincidence, and rather an unlucky one in this instance," he replied.

"A remarkable coincidence, too, is it not, that just after you got rich we should become poor? It must mean something, I think."

"It means that fortune is a fickle goddess; that she capriciously takes away to-day the favors she bestowed yesterday; that she is fond of surprises, and turns smiles into tears, and *vice versa*, just for the fun of the thing."

"She is a good deal like myself. I believe I should do the same thing for pure mischief, if I had the power."

"Then you cannot so much blame the fitful old dame. Ethel, did you know I have decided to form one of your party?"

"Really and truly, Mr. Ferrol?" and Ethel rushed up to him, warmly grasping his hand.

"Really and truly! Are you not sorry?"

"I am delighted! Our only regret was in leaving you. What a happy company! When did you decide?"

"Five minutes ago."

"Does mamma know it?"

"Not yet. Will you ask her if I may go?"

"I will be the first to tell her the good news," and away sped the happy girl.

Mrs. Forsyth received the news with less exhibition of rejoicing than had Ethel, though her cheek flushed a little, and a light came in her eyes.

"Why, mamma, you take it as a matter of course, and as though it were to be expected! I am greatly elated. You see, it just makes us three-times-three; we are all even."

"How is that, Ethel? What mean you?"

"Well, Mr. and Mrs. Braun, and Basil—three; Mrs. Willoughby, Francisco and Beatrice—three; Mr. Ferrol, you, mamma, and I—three. Isn't there a calculation for you?"

A general laugh followed, Mr. and Mrs. Braun, beside Mrs. Willoughby, being present.

"More of a calculation than you yourself suspect, I imagine, Miss Ethel," remarked Mr. Braun.

"I fail to see that I have said anything to excite all this laughter. I will repeat it to Mr. Ferrol, and ask him; I wonder if he will laugh, too!"

Away Ethel ran, scarce hearing, not heeding, her mother's "Ethel!"

Mr. Ferrol listened attentively, and, rather to Ethel's surprise, laughed heartily.

"And you do really see something to laugh at?" interrogated innocent Ethel.

"I have never given you credit for being a mathematician; it seems you are not that only, but you are something else peculiar to your sex, more peculiar to elderly matrons than to maidens."

"You speak in riddles, Mr. Ferrol. Do explain yourself!"

"You would not understand; you do not comprehend yourself this morning."

"I comprehend one thing, which is, that I am disgusted with old people. I will hie to the young folks."

All affairs, trifling or otherwise, were arranged on that day, preparatory to an early departure in the morning.

Faithful Rachel stood by her friends, declaring she had entered Mrs. Forsyth's service for life, and would, therefore, follow her to the end of the world, were she bent on such a freak as to go.

Susan also, a little maid of all work, who had been invaluable during the last year, begged to be allowed still to form one of the family.

Rachel objected, insisting Susan was "no 'count," "wasn't worth her salt," "would be only a hindrance," and so forth. Mrs. Willoughby, however, took the girl as her own assistant, finding her of great use already in cleansing and packing the clothing which had become utterly demoralized in its hasty flitting from the flames.

Thus Rachel and Susan were forced to a still longer companionship, and each apparently had resolved to be peaceable and make the best of it.

"We are a caravan, that is what we are, or a cavalcade," decided Ethel, when well under way.

"You will think we are a caravan when we join scores of travelers upon the plains. We are in for a long journey after we shall leave Claremont. Please tell us when you get tired of it, and we will set you down by the way," kindly promised Francisco.

"You know I am the last one you would leave by the way, my good cousin. You couldn't get along without me."

"Couldn't we, though? How did we manage to come all the way up into this part of the North Pole?" questioned Francisco.

"O, you did not know me then. Do you remember, cousin, when you first saw me, feeding chickens?" My poor little flock! They will never see me more. Do you suppose they will know the difference betwixt the young Smalleys and myself?"

"That depends on whether the young Smalleys shower down before their admiring eyes and ever-hungry beaks the similar quantity and quality of cornmeal and other provisions which their former mistress was accustomed to do."

"And you have no idea that they had the least attachment to myself personally, and that they will not miss me—myself?"

"On the contrary, I think they *may* prefer the Smalleys; that is, if they may be supposed to have the least choice in the matter.

"You were an autocrat to your chickens. They presumed upon no familiarities. Whereas in their present more homily place the half-dozen young owners of the brood will sit down in their midst, and be quite at home. There, too, will be pigs and cows; your chickens will find themselves in their proper place."

And thus during this first day's journey Ethel spoke of things of the past, which indicated that it was with some tenderness, if not regret, she bade adieu to all which could remind her of her former life.

The discourse of Basil and Beatrice was more of the future. The mind of the former was full of interest and curiosity as to the land he was bound for. And Beatrice, a dear lover of her home and native land, wearied not in not only replying to his questions, but discoursing at length upon what she thought would please him.

The party remained a few days at Claremont to complete some preparations, as also to enjoy and profit by the Sunday services at St. Patrick's. They put up at the hotel where Mr. Ferrol had been stopping, word having been sent to the priest of their arrival.

The latter lost no time in paying his respects, and he was filled with astonishment when he listened to the multiplicity of strange incidents which had taken place since the departure of his friends for Sunapee but three days ago.

Ere this, however, Father English had schooled himself to be surprised at little that occurs, so passing strange are passages of each one's life.

When he learned of the influence those incidents were to have upon the conduct of Mr. Ferrol and Mrs. Forsyth, he was affected more deeply. He had hoped that the new converts would make Claremont their home, and that for the future he would have some more congenial society; now this hope must prove vain.

However, this priest was one of those who calculate very little upon what *may* happen; he was one of those disciplined souls who give up the dearest schemes and hopes (if they allow themselves to have any) without a murmur, being altogether submissive to the Divine Will. He was particularly pleased that he was able to confer a favor upon Mr. Ferrol before his final departure, although this very favor was one entirely opposed to a different one which he had anticipated.

Saturday afternoon had come around. It had been arranged that all should go to confession on that day. The three young Catholics were, therefore, in retreat for several hours, while Basil, the black sheep, as he had styled himself, took that opportunity of banishment to indulge in his somewhat neglected favorite amusement of fishing.

Mr. and Mrs. Braun, enjoying again a second honeymoon, had kept themselves somewhat isolated. Mrs. Willoughby and Mrs. Forsyth were still continuing their after-dinner conversation upon the balcony. Mr. Ferrol, who had some time since left them, again returned, appearing somewhat uneasy and constrained.

Quick to perceive, Mrs. Willoughby made her excuses and withdrew, supposing simply the gentleman had some unfinished business relations with her sister which he might wish to complete. Such, indeed, was the case.

Mr. Ferrol, with unusual tact and delicacy, explained to Mrs. Forsyth that, with her permission, he was about to settle upon her and her daughter one half of his fortune. Mrs. Forsyth raised her hands in deprecation. Unheeding this, Mr. Ferrol said in more authoritative tones than he had ever before spoken to the lady:

"Consider, my friend; by accepting this from me, you lay yourself under no obligations. You are as my sister: look upon me as your brother, you who have no brother. There should be no scruple upon your part —allow me to say there must be none. In all our relations heretofore, pardon me the allusion, you have dictated as was your right, and I have submitted, as in duty bound. In this which I now propose I am the dictator, and I beg you to submit gracefully and graciously.

"You cannot help but know, my friend, that I honor and revere you above all women. To know you, was to love you, and to love you was to approach nearer your plane of goodness and truth. I owe you much. Money cannot repay the debt. All that I have would be too little; accept then the trifle that I offer. It is your own, my dearest friend."

Mrs. Forsyth was visibly affected. With difficulty she restrained her tears. Her voice trembled as she said:

"God knows how it has been between you and me, Mr. Ferrol. You have been the kindest, the noblest of friends. I needed not this fresh proof of your generosity, of your friendly interest, of your unselfish devotion. If I have hitherto been unkind and appeared to you ungrateful——"

"Not in the least, poor child—I have never for one moment blamed you," was Mr. Ferrol's assurance.

"I was bound up in 'Bird'snest'—I was fettered and enthralled with old associations and the memory of old loves. I had become morbid, sensitive to change, either outwardly or interiorly. The loss of my home and means of living has disenchanted me. Were 'Bird'snest' standing I should not be here. The shock of these late events has not only rent asunder the bonds which held me, as I thought, irrevocably to the past, but has opened my eyes and my heart to a new light and a not impossible peace—— You will not suspect me of mercenary motives, you cannot do so after your munificent bequest——"

"You surely know me better, my friend—you should know the truth as it is, that I would lay down my life for you! Have I not thrice been rejected? And still have you dwelt in my heart of hearts. Even now would I a fourth time offer you my hand in marriage, but to save your feelings; there would be no humiliation in a refusal from *you*, my friend."

Lois Forsyth arose and knelt at his feet. She bowed her head slightly, as if for his blessing, and murmured:

"You know I would not say it were it not the truth—I am yours, my friend."

At last—at last—Mr. Ferrol struggled manfully with his tears, the first he had wept since he was a boy.

The following day the bans were published, the first intelligence to any one of the party that such an event as a marriage was contemplated.

Such a surprise as this, eclipsing all the other unexpected things which had followed in such rapid succession, was too much to have been experienced at so solemn a place as before the altar. At least it may be fairly ventured that Ethel heard very little of Father English's sermon.

Returning to their rooms, among many other remarks which were made, Mr. Braun said to Ethel:

"Your little example in multiplication, your 'three-times-three,' Miss Ethel, was spoken in a spirit of prophecy the other day, was it not?" Ethel looked up inquiringly, then a smile broke over her face.

"You begin to see now where the laugh came in—all right."

Like Basil at the finding of his father, Ethel resolved the question—was she glad or sorry? Her heart answered yes—and she went up frankly to him she had ever known as her mother's friend, and, placing her hand in his, said playfully: "Nearer and dearer papa Ferrol."

The daughter expressed surprise that her mother was to be married in her plain traveling dress that was still unfinished at the dressmaker's. In truth, there was no end to surprises, and each one was speculating as to what possibly might come next.

It had been decided they should set out on their long journey Wednesday morning, that being the earliest that the ladies' wardrobes could be procured. This, then, was the morning for the marriage to take place, at Low Mass, at the early hour of six. The night preceding this another incident happened:

From Ethel's room, in the dead of night, a piercing shriek was heard, resounding through the house.

Every inmate was startled.

A hurrying throng gathered in the halls, but, of course, only the friends of the young lady entered her room, which was shared also by Beatrice.

"Oh, that horrid cat! that horrid cat!" was all the explanation she could give of her fright. She was found sitting upright in her bed, her eyes wildly staring, her face contorted with fear. Beatrice was vainly endeavoring to pacify her.

"It must have been a dream," said the latter to her mother and aunt, as those ladies hurriedly entered.

"A dream?" shrieked Ethel, almost in hysterics. "Look under the bed; it is under the bed, that horrid cat, with the biggest head, and the frightfulest yell—O mamma, do not let it fly at you!"

"My child, there is nothing under the bed. What made you think it was there?"

"I saw it, and I heard its steps; it must be under the bed, or it may have hidden somewhere."

Thorough search was made throughout the room, but no sign of the object of Ethel's fright.

Uninterested occupants of other rooms, disgusted that a foolish girl's dream had thus disturbed them, with smiles or rather frowns of scorn again swiftly retired.

But Ethel would not permit her friends to retire until they had assisted her to see with her own eyes that there was nothing like a cat visible anywhere.

Reassured at length, Ethel, weak and weary, prepared again to lie down.

"It must have been a cat's ghost," she said.

"You may be sure it was a dream," insisted her mother, bidding her good-night.

"A dream!" repeated Ethel; "I saw it with my own eyes, and I heard it with my ears, and I was never so driven wild with fright."

The following morning, reflecting upon the same in the light of day, the whole thing appeared to her differently, and she reluctantly admitted to herself—it must have been a dream.

CHAPTER XXV.

SUNAPEE TALKS OF THE MARRIAGE WHILE OUR FRIENDS JOURNEY SOUTHWARD.

MADAME RUMOR flew with her usual swiftness, telling the Sunapeeians and the Duxburyites of the marriage of the late rector of St. Mark's with the late widow of "Bird's-nest." This was but a consummation of the universal impression of the fitness of things; great had been the marvel that such an event had not before occurred. Having been for years abandoned, the idea had again prevailed since the misfortunes of Mrs. Forsyth. That the rector had been always devoted to her, and that she had again and again refused him, was as well known as if it had been proclaimed by the gentleman himself from his own pulpit. The number, however, of these proposals and rejections had become indefinitely multiplied by time and travel; but that it would once more occur was fully believed. How else, was argued, were Mrs. Forsyth and her daughter, who had lived in ease and comfort all their days, to get along in the world for a single month? Also, the fact that Mr. Ferrol had as suddenly become wealthy seemed to be a special providence in favor of the widow.

Therefore, for the space of a day, a topic was furnished for loungers upon corners. For an equal or longer space the proverbially longer tongue of woman had this sweet morsel to roll. An infinite number of visits were exchanged. The more precise housekeeper hurried off her children to school, lullabied her baby to sleep, arranged her breakfast dishes, bright and shining, upon the shelves, swept and dusted in an incredibly brief time, thinking to go out to her neighbor's to gossip upon the one theme. Her less particular neighbor, however, is ahead of her, and comes rushing in, having left her dishes stacked in the pan and her house looking "four ways for Sunday."

"Don't it beat all!" she exclaims, breathlessly, taking it for granted that her neighbor is posted. "Notwithstanding we have always known it would be some time, and have prophesied it time without number, it has come so sudden-like, it has took me all aback; hasn't it you?"

"Well, yes; I didn't think it would come off quite so soon; but I suppose they thought it better to marry before they went on their journey. They do say Mrs. Forsyth didn't have more than money enough to take her there; but I suppose Mrs. Willoughby is rich, and could have given her a home."

"As it was Mrs. Forsyth, I should thought she'd 've waited awhile, just for the speech o' people."

"Why, what do you mean?"

"For fear they'd say she married him just for his money. It does look that way, now, don't it?"

At this point came in another, who lived right across the way; and this was no other than Mrs. Huldah Towne, whose one particular friend was the precise housekeeper. It was to the house of Mrs. Huldah that the latter had been preparing to go when stopped short by the entrance of Mrs. Slack, who, as we have said, left her dishes in an unwashed stack.

"Don't you think so, Mrs. Towne?" inquired Mrs. Slack, the latest speaker.

"Think what—about what?"

"That people will say Mrs. Forsyth married Mr. Ferrol just for his money, having refused him so many times when he was poor, you know?"

"What does Mrs. Forsyth care about what people say? Not that"—vigorously snapping her fingers. "They may say it, and they do say it; and what if they do?" continued Mrs. Huldah, who still kept the floor. "Mr. and Mrs. Ferrol will go on their way rejoicing just the same; and, for my own part, I am glad they are married, and I wish them well. I can read Mrs. Forsyth like a book. A good little soul, but odd, rather, and living in herself. She worshiped Paul Forsyth as if he had been a god. When he died he didn't die to her. When her father died he still lived at 'Bird's-nest'—to her. She 'was wedded to her idols,' like Ephraim of old, and just wanted to be let alone. The fire broke the charm, and let her loose from all them things. There was nothing left but Mr. Ferrol, and in rebounding from such a shock she struck him; you see, she had liked him all along; she had depended on him; he had been more to her than she knew; she got her eyes opened, and, of course, when Mr. Ferrol asked her again to be his wife, as everybody knew he would do, she was ready to say yes; and I'm glad. It's nobody's business; it's a special providence."

"I thought that was the view you would take of it," said her friend, approvingly.

"But do you really believe Mrs. Forsyth would have married him if he hadn't come into all this money?" inquired doubtful Mrs. Slack.

"Indeed I do—yes. Mr. Ferrol can always make a living, and he is a model man."

"You didn't think so once," reminded Mrs. Slack.

"Well, yes, I know; but Mr. Ferrol and I have both grown wiser since then. Any way, *he* has. He don't seem the same man he did fifteen years ago. He hasn't a bit of that pride and self-conceit, and none of them lordly airs. Dear me! he wouldn't look at you fifteen years ago, and now he is as sociable and friendly as you please."

"And his money didn't make him any different, did it?" inquired Mrs. Slack.

"Not a particle."

"What an awful pity he got to be a Papist!"

"Not a bit! hasn't a man a right to be what he's a mind? Who do you suppose knows best—you or Mr. Ferrol? He's a learn'd man. He's studied up the whole thing. He believed in it, or else he wouldn't have given up his place and been ready to brave poverty and working with his hands. And Providence rewarded his boldness and courage. That's the way to look at it. I'm for fair play and justice."

"You always did take up on the wrong side," asserted Mrs. Slack.

"On the wrong side—how?"

"Agin everybody else. You won't find ten folks in Sunapee and in Duxbury put together that will talk as you do about it."

"All right. Am I obliged to speak different from what I believe because a few hundred idiots, without an atom of charity, say what I would cut out my tongue for saying? The good sense of the town has departed from it. Henceforth I'll hold my tongue," and Mrs. Huldah, inviting her particular friend to come over, left suddenly.

"You may allers know where *she* is—jes contrary to where everybody else is," said Mrs. Slack, rising to go.

"Well, I'm with her every time; she always knows what she is talking about, has an opinion of her own, and don't veer with every weather-cock," responded the better housekeeper.

"O, I knew ye was the best of friends, but I thought on this matter——"

"I agree with Mrs. Towne"—and here the parting civilities were exchanged.

Thus was discussed the subject of the marriage, which had taken place quietly at Claremont, according to the ceremonials prescribed by the Church for that holy Sacrament.

* * * * *

The long journey of many weeks, from the white hills of New Hampshire, through tunnels and across rivers, over mountain and vale, by railroad, thence by stage-coach or on the backs of burros over desolate plains covered with sage bush, or winding around mountains whose lofty tops glistened with snow—was one long to be remembered by our party of "three-times-three." At least, of the nine, two were unwearied and ever interested. We need not say these were Ethel and Basil. Francisco and Beatrice were longing for home. The companionship of their young friends lent a charm to the journey, but the end could not come too soon.

They were delighted to make a halt of a few days at

Trinidad, a rising town in Colorado, whose guardian mount they had been watching from afar. Here visits were made to the Convent of the Sisters of Loretto (the mother house of which was at Santa Fé), where Beatrice met more than one whom she had formerly known. To visit a convent was a novelty to our Northern friends. We need hardly say they were surprised and delighted at everything.

The church was under the care of some Jesuit Fathers, who were Italians, though speaking pretty good English. The friends remained over Sunday, and, of course, went to Mass. Here was where Ethel first saw a few persons wearing shawls over the heads and kneeling upon the floor during all the ceremonies. It will be remembered Francisco had referred to the multitude who follow this custom in the Church of St. Francis, at Santa Fé.

From Trinidad was no considerable town until they arrived at Los Vegas—the meadows. This town was in New Mexico, and our party needed only their eyes to assure them they were in a foreign country, even though it was a territory annexed to our own. The compact city, built around a *p'àza* or square, consisting of long, one-story buildings, every room of which opened on one side upon the street, on the other upon a small inner court yard, surprised them not so much as did the people, the animals and the way of doing things. However, we as a story-teller need not loiter to speak minutely of these things. A railroad will now conduct you, gentle reader, to the health-giving town we speak of in "the twinkling of an eye" compared to the toilsome journey we are speaking of, and you can go and see how it is yourself. Do not forget to go out some half dozen

miles to the hot springs, which are now made ready for
invalids and pleasure tourists, but which, at the time
we are referring to, were only beginning to attract attention.

Our party did not visit these springs, but they went
down to another Convent of Loretto, and to the College
of the Jesuit Fathers. They thought Los Vegas interesting, but were quite willing to start early one Monday
morning for Santa Fé, which was now less than one
hundred miles distant. They had considered themselves almost home, particularly those who had traveled the ground before; but how long the way drew
itself out! All were very weary when the hills which
shut in Santa Fé appeared in view.

"And we are about to enter the promised land," cried
Ethel to Francisco.

"*Deo Gratias!*" responded the young man, devoutly.

"*Deo Gratias!*" repeated Beatrice, with a solemn inclination of the head.

"I might say the same, only *my* promised land is a
few hundred miles down further, for which I am sorry
enough," and Basil sighed, uttering these words, knowing well that here, after a few days of rest, must come
his parting with Beatrice.

CHAPTER XXVI.

YOUTHFUL LOVERS—CROSSES AND CROWNS.

MRS. WILLOUGHBY'S house was commodiously large, and she insisted that her sister-in-law should make her home with her. Mr. Ferrol rather objected at first. He had his fancies of a quiet home all his own, and this he was resolved to have as soon as possible. For the present, however, they were welcome guests at the lovely home of Mrs. Willoughby.

During her absence the house and grounds had been well kept. As far as the eye could see the servants had been faithful to their trust.

Ethel was overflowing with delight.

"It is almost as beautiful as 'Bird'snest,' and on a much larger scale. My dear cousins, why did you not tell me more about this fine place of yours, especially as you were not expecting me ever to behold it. I intend never to return to New Hampshire. They will have to dispense with my presence from the annual patriotic celebration and the camp-meeting. I am always to stay here. You remained away a whole year—how could you?"

"We found such excellent company in the blue-eyed young lady, who doted on chickens and kittens. By the way, those blue eyes of yours are a novelty down here. Be careful how you break the hearts of our susceptible young men, who have yet to see blue eyes and golden hair. They will mistake you for an angel." This said Francisco.

"And you think that would be a very great mistake?" interrogated Ethel.

Francisco looked his cousin steadily in the eye, and responded:

"If I say yes, I flatter you: if I say no, I offend you. I will leave the question to be answered by those who have not known you so long as I."

"Cruel, cruel Francisco! what an insinuation is that! You know from experience that I am no angel! I think it must be very sweet to be called an angel—do you not think so, Beatrice?"

Now Beatrice had heard Basil whisper that word in her ear and it had not pleased her. Her response to Ethel was:

"You are jesting, Ethel, but I will answer seriously. No, I would not like such a name applied to me; as I think you mean it. I believe there are angels on earth; but they have no wings, dress in black, and are known as Sisters. I would like to be worthy a place among them."

"Dear little Beatrice, and you will be. You carry the marks of your calling—I shall pity poor Basil—the Sisters do not marry, I think, you said."

"O no; they are brides of Christ," whispered Beatrice. Ethel said no more, but fell to thinking. Presently she said:

"It is strange, but I have not seen a single priest married. Every one is an old bachelor. Mr. Ferrol was never married, and I did not think it so strange to find housekeepers everywhere. They *can* marry, cannot they.

Francisco and Beatrice joined in a hearty laugh.

"Have you only just now made a study of that subject?" inquired Beatrice.

"How long a time, think you, before you will have learned all that our Church has to teach of faith and practice? A long time, indeed, and you will be surprised ere you come to the end of the great lesson," rejoined Francisco.

"But you have not answered my question," spoke Ethel, in a low tone.

She was recalling to mind her own impressions and predictions with regard to Francisco, and the remark of Beatrice upon one occasion referring to Francisco's vocation. From many trifling incidents, also, she was quite aware that it was understood that her beloved cousin should become a priest, although great delicacy had been observed in any inadvertent reference to it. It was Beatrice who replied:

"Like the Sisters they are devoted to God, and wedded only to the Church."

Ethel stood as if transfixed. Her dilated eyes looked straight forward, and a spot of flame burned in either cheek, while otherwise her face wore the lily's pallor.

"Why, what see you, cousin Ethel?" exclaimed both cousins at once, looking in the direction toward which her eyes were fastened, expecting to behold some horror.

"Only a ghost," answered Ethel, in an unnatural, strained voice, and with a forced laugh she turned and fled from the garden, where all had been standing, to her room. She locked the door and stood still wringing her hands.

Poor Ethel, it had come upon her so suddenly. Her adored Francisco, whom she had loved at first sight, whom she had prized and treasured from day to day in her heart of hearts, till he was dearer than life itself an hundred fold!

How was she to bear this great grief—this demolishment of her idol, before which she might no more bow down and worship?

It was all explained now. Francisco had been manly, dignified, reserved, but polite and kind in all his intercourse with her. There had been nothing of the lover; and this same fact had but intensified her admiration and devotion. She had given her love unsought as a child, as a maiden; now, in this last hour she had awakened to womanhood, to foresee in the distance but a shadowed vista, where every flower was blighted and every star bedimmed.

In this one hour of her life the new religion, instead of comforting, appeared to her as the very source of her misery. It was the merciless tyrant forcing the barbed arrow in her heart. It was the harsh masters imposing self-denials and penances—the iron hand showering incense over the withered hopes and dead emotions that had been crushed through a selfish power, despotic and absolute.

It is unnecessary to follow Ethel through this fiery ordeal. Those souls which are destined to become great or strong have first to be subjected to this fire, in one form or another.

The stern purifier had come early to Ethel Forsyth. Nor winds nor clouds had given warning, but in the bright sunshine of the morn, whose sky was blue and fair, had fallen the bolt! What marvel she was stunned, and hurt, and scarred for life! Both brother and sister divined the cause of Ethel's emotion.

"Poor Ethel," commiserated Beatrice. After a minute of silence Francisco said:

"Beneath a surface, light and foamy, Ethel's nature has a depth hitherto unfathomed. She will come out all right, and I predict for her a noble womanhood;" and he wandered away by himself, murmuring as he went, "Poor Ethel!"

Ethel fought her battle alone, by word giving no token of the conflict within her. In the meantime, after a day or two, during which she kept her room under the feminine plea of headache, she resumed her old manner toward all the household. She became blithe and gay, much to the pleasure of her cousins, and appeared interested in all that was devised for the enjoyment of all.

The churches were all visited—and to St. Francis the whole household gathered every morning for early Mass.

The hills were searched for flowers, old Fort Marcy and the modern military headquarters were explored, the convent, the Sister's Hospital, the Archbishop's garden, the Manderfield Place, the Home of the Johnsons, blooming in mid-luxuriance of flower and fruit, all were visited with more or less delight.

The Brauns had still lingered, Basil's mother needing rest.

The time came, however, for the breaking up of the party.

"We find ourselves compelled to make a break in your favorite fragment of the multiplication table, Miss Ethel. You can do as I was made to do when a boy, say the table backwards. It was *three times-three* when you made your remarkable prophecy. We will leave you to rehearse your lesson of two-times-three, while we go down the Rio Grandé singing once three is three." Ethel responded to Mr. Braun:

"You have great reason to rejoice over your portion of the song. You must be thinking yourself the hero of a novel. Were I a girl of genius now, I would put you in a book."

"O, deliver me from such an embalmment."

"You do not aspire then to that kind of immortality?"

"No; I desire to drown the romance of my life, in memory of the present blessed reality. A year from now you will all come down to my home in the valley, where we will find ourselves again the happy three-times-three."

Before leaving, Basil was brave, and told his love to Beatrice.

"We are so young—we are children yet," objected Beatrice.

"Nonsense," answered Basil, "I am nineteen, in my twentieth year; you are scarcely three years younger. I have learned that in this country people marry in their teens."

"I am not through school yet," urged the maiden.

"O well, you can go to school for a year, I shall be twenty then. I love you, Beatrice. Cannot you say to me, "I love you, Basil?""

The maiden's eyes were downcast; she made no response.

"That is all I want now, Beatrice; we are to be separated for one long year; if you will only say those four little words, little but mighty, I will go away content."

"There is a reason why I should not say them," she at length replied, raising to his her candid eyes.

"Why?"

And still she did not answer.

"I cannot believe you are like some girls we read of, who love to flirt, who seek to win a fellow's heart and then scornfully reject and tread upon it," continued Basil.

"Basil!" came reproachfully from the maiden's lips, while her eyes raised to his filled with tears.

"Forgive me, my only love. I said rightly that I could not believe thus of you, nor do I for one single moment. I know you to be sincere and true. Your name, *Beatrice*, signifying happy, is to me a synonym for truth. I not only love you, I respect and reverence you."

She put up her hand deprecatingly.

"You express far more than I merit; you see in me what I *would* be; for I must tell you, Basil, that from my earliest girlhood my aspirations have been for a religious life."

Not comprehending her meaning, Basil responded:

"You are very religious already; and, though I am not so now, I must inevitably become so under your influence and example. I should never interfere with your devotions; and I regard your piety as your encompassing grace."

"Perhaps you do not understand what I mean by 'religious life'—it is that of the convent. I would be a Sister, like good Sister Catherine."

"And Sisters never marry?"

"They are brides of Christ," repeated Beatrice, as already she had explained to Ethel.

"And hide yourself in a convent and break my heart, Beatrice?"

We will no farther pursue this conversation, which terminated in mystification and irresolution upon the part of Beatrice, and in a determined will in Basil to "conquer or to die," as he resolutely expressed himself.

The young man congratulated himself upon having revealed his love to Beatrice, for he foresaw that had he kept silence until another year it would have been too late. The convent might have won her. He resolved upon bringing everything possible to bear on shaking Beatrice's "aspirations." She was a sweet and docile child, thought Basil, loved to gratify her friends, was ready for any self-denial, and surely it would be no difficult matter to bring her over! He had taken her by surprise; when she should come to reflect upon his words, her own heart would prompt her to decide according to his wishes. Basil had not confessed his love unadvisedly. He had studied the subject and had watched and studied Beatrice. He had seen her eye brighten and her cheek flush at his unexpected coming. From repeated observations he saw himself more favored than her own beloved brother. He had been careful to note all these things, because he felt conscious of how much he had at stake. With all the might of his strong nature he loved Beatrice. The affection was altogether different from the brotherly attachment with which Ethel had inspired him. The simple fact that Beatrice had heretofore aspired to the "Sisterhood" appeared not so strange a thing to Basil, considering that the convent had been so much her home. It would not be difficult, certainly not insurmountable, to combat her objections. Much surprised, then, was Basil at the pertinacity with which Beatrice adhered to her first statement. He was astonished to find in her so much persistence of purpose. He began to wonder if, after all, he had been mistaken in supposing that Beatrice returned his sentiment. He hastened to assure himself.

"Am I asking too much when I ask you to inform me if I am repulsive or hateful to you?" he coolly inquired of the object of his devotion.

"Can you ask such a question?" was the reproachful response of Beatrice.

"Remember, please, you are at perfect liberty to answer or not to answer any questions I may propose to you. You will forgive my impertinence, if such you deem it. I am not repulsive, then, to you. Do you regard me in the light of a brother—as you regard Francisco, for instance?"

"I would prefer not to answer," said Beatrice.

"Please say yes or no, my dear friend. If you have no different feeling towards me than that you cherish for your brother, then I will not bother you; I will say good-bye and hie to the other end of creation. I am up and down in my notions of things. I would scorn to plead for love of any girl if it had not already sprang to me spontaneously as mine to her. In a word, as I asked you first, 'Do you love me, Beatrice?'"

"Yes, I love you, Basil."

"All right! It has taken a good many days and a good many words to bring it to the surface; but I have it now—that's all I want, my darling!"

"But I ought not to love you—I must not; that I do is what makes me unhappy."

"Unhappy? And belie your name? O, no, my Beatrice!"

Poor Beatrice felt unequal to the task of convincing Basil that she could never be his, and that she must be the bride of the Church, and so allowed him to go on with his raptures. At the earliest opportunity, however, she conversed with her mother upon the subject, urging her to speak with Basil and convince him of the futility of any further pleading.

"My child," returned the mother, "this is a matter of your own decision finally. But before you arrive at that point, time, reflection and prayer are necessary. The fact that you have long meditated becoming a religious is not proof of a vocation. Have you consulted Father Fiólon?"

"I have not seen him since Basil told me—since he talked to me in this way," responded the daughter, confusedly.

"Mr. Braun's family will leave in a few days. I honor and respect them highly. Were I to choose for you, my child, Basil should be your companion for life: unless, indeed, you have a calling for that higher life, before which every other inclination must be silent. I advise you to see the priest without delay; he will be the better judge."

No time was lost in placing the matter before Father Fiélon.

Having listened to Beatrice, who spoke to him with all the freedom she had spoken to her mother, the priest said:

"You have a strong friendship for this young man; you regard him with more affectionate interest than any other person?"

"I do, Father."

"But he is not a Catholic?"

"Not yet, Father. His parents are of our Faith, and he is ready to embrace it."

"Why does he not do so? He has had plenty of time since his arrival to have made some advances in the right direction."

"I think he is waiting to be approached upon the subject."

"Cannot you solicit him to come to me? Before I give consent to your union with any young gentleman, I desire to make a more thorough personal acquaintance, and to see him received into the Church."

"But, Father, I did not say to you that I wished to accept Basil's——" she hesitated.

"What, then, do you wish, my child?"

"Did I not say that from my childhood I have wished to give my whole heart unto God, and to become one of the dear Sisters of Loretto? I thought you knew that, Father."

"A great many young girls entertain such a desire for a period—that is very well; but it seems you have allowed your heart to wander in another direction; you are not, therefore, free to engage according to your previous fancies."

"Were they only fancies, Father?"

"They might have been. At all events a suspicion, a doubt, has come over you."

"Hardly so, Father. I came to you fully resolved to forget Basil and to have you inform him to that effect; and for myself, at once to enter upon my novitiate, if you deem it expedient, Father."

"And why, Beatrice, my daughter?"

"Because I ought to do so. It would be deserting my Creator for a creature. It would be leaving Almighty God for a mortal man!"

"All very fine, my dear child. Then it is from a sense of duty you would do this?"

"From a sense of duty, Father."

"Then had you not previously cherished this idea of a religious life, you would have felt free to have said yes to young Braun?"

"Yes, Father."

"And you wish to hear what I sincerely and truly think about all this?"

"I intend to abide by your decision, Father."

"Very well; send the young man to me."

The young man, however, had thought the thing over, and had resolved that the wisest course for him was to intercede with Mrs. Willoughby and the priest, also. While Beatrice had been at the house of the priest, Basil had been pleading his cause before Mrs. Willoughby. It happened, therefore, that as Beatrice passed over the threshold to go out, Basil passed over to go in to Father Fiélon's. Bowing and smiling, they passed each other without a word.

The priest kept Basil a long time in conversation. Like every one else, he was pleased with him. He found him ready and eager to make a study of Catholicity, and likewise discovered in him such germs of native nobility and manliness as quite drew him to his heart. Accordingly, when Basil bowed himself out from the Reverend presence, he felt a consciousness that if the power lay with the priest his case was won.

At her next interview with Father Fiélon, Beatrice became disenchanted of her childish dream for the one life, and resolved to accept the Sacrament of Marriage. The convincing argument by which her scruples and her sense of duty were overcome was something like this from the lips of her spiritual director:

"Persons mistake in supposing that in order to serve God they must devote themselves especially to Him in the Sacrament of Holy Order. Persons in the world may serve God acceptably and save their own souls. Few out of the many are called to that higher life of which St. Paul speaks. Pious women have become mothers of religious doctors and saints. Through their sacred maternity have they recommended themselves unto the Father, and to the Son, and to the Mother of Christ. The faithful wife, the conscientious mother, the Christian neighbor, the true and loving woman as mistress of a family, has more calls for the practice of self-denial, for patience, forbearance, and all Christian virtues, than any other of God's creatures.

"When the bride stands before the altar, could her eye penetrate the future she would stand appalled, or, fainting, would withdraw her hand from his to whom she plights her undying troth. Happily, no hand unrolls the scroll, and her warm affection and lively fancy lend *coleur de rose* to a long, happy hereafter.

"That young maiden who is grounded in her religious faith, when she enters upon the solemn marriage state does so with all that prayerful consideration as does the novice when she takes the veil. In the heart of each should be perfect love to God, faith and trust in Him above all others, an expectation to be guided by Him, all subservient to a spirit of complete submission to the Divine will. A mind thus disciplined will bear bravely, even cheerfully, burdens, crosses and disappointments in either a wedded or single state."

"You surprise me, Father. I had supposed that

those who have taken the vows of a religious are nearer and dearer to the Divine Heart. We read of those who 'follow the Lamb whithersoever He goeth.'"

"Yes, but there are many who have lived exposed to all the distractions and temptations of the world who have led lives as pious and truly Christian as those whom the cloister has sheltered. Look at the mother of St. Augustine. The Church would not have had this great saint had she reckoned Monica among her precious Sisterhood. I once was acquainted with a woman who lived to see her five sons anointed for the priesthood. Was not that glory enough, and the greatest? and was she not serving her heavenly Father by brightening and polishing the jewels He had given her for the Master's crown of rejoicing?"

"Why, then, should any one choose a religious life?"

"Why did you not choose it?"

"I thought I did—I do not know——"

"No; you may know you did not fully choose it, or that God had called you for something else, or your heart would not have gone to Basil Braun, even against and without your will."

"You think, then, I have no vocation?"

"I think decidedly that you have a vocation to become the good and faithful wife of Basil Braun in about one year from this time; I shall then expect to unite you to him in the bonds of holy marriage, with the blessing of the Church; now you may go and tell him that you have given up one brief dream for one more lasting. *Deo benedicite.*"

The priest thus expressed himself to the young girl for two reasons: one of these was, he truly thought it better for her ultimately to make the choice which he recommended; the other to try her, in order to ascertain if her fancied vocation was truly a call from heaven. If the latter should prove true, and God had really called her, then his words would have little effect upon her, because the voice of God would be mightier than the voice of man. If, after all that he had said, Beatrice should come back to him and say: "Another voice than yours, Father, says to me, 'Come'—a voice which I dare not (nor would you counsel me to) disobey"—then would he be convinced and offer no further plea for Basil.

Francisco was to go down with the Brauns as far as Albuquerqué, where he was again to take up his abode with the Jesuit Fathers, perhaps permanently. It was finally agreed upon by all parties that at this college of the Jesuits should be left Basil for a series of months, in order that he might not only sooner acquire the Spanish language, but be thoroughly instructed in Christian doctrine. Therefore it was that the parting of Basil and Beatrice was hopeful and satisfactory. Basil had asked only for a mere expression of the love of Beatrice. He gained that and more—the promise of her hand at the expiration of a year. Mrs. Braun, more healthful and happy, parted gayly from her friends, and went with her husband to his home in the Rio Grandé Valley.

CHAPTER XXVII.

CONFESSION OF OCTAVE GEOFFRION—MARRIAGE BELLS —WHITE VEIL.

IF we have said little or nothing of Mr. Ferrol and his bride, it is not because of shame or sensitiveness at their hasty marriage. They were old enough to pass their honeymoon without our hypercritical observations; likewise it is enough to say that they so circumspectly carried themselves during their journey and subsequent tarrying at Mrs. Willoughby's as to be mistaken for people who had been married for years instead of days. Neither Mr. Ferrol nor his wife regretted the change in their relations; and Mrs. Ferrol was one of the few brides who might have looked into the future, even standing before the altar, without flinching or fainting.

Mr. Ferrol was not slow in selecting grounds and building a house, which was ready for occupancy early in the spring.

In the absence of the young men, Ethel and Beatrice became still more intimate friends. They entered the convent school as day pupils, remaining at home except for recitations. A great change came gradually over Ethel. In a measure she lost her volatility, became thoughtful, and devoted much time to reading. Her former abhorrence—a book—had become a frequent and beloved companion. She sought acquaintance with the Sisters, and became fond of lingering within the shadows of the towers and trees of the Convent of Loretto.

A hasty messenger came one day to Mrs. Willoughby. He bore a summons for her immediate attendance at the death-bed of her cousin, Octave Geoffrion. This cousin for several months had been absent from Santa Fé. The invitation to repair to his sick-room was the first intimation the lady had received of his return. Accompanying the messenger on his return, Mrs. Willoughby learned from him that only on the previous evening had Octave Geoffrion arrived in the city. He had been borne on a litter from the mountains. Arriving at the house, which had been the home of her own childhood, she was met by Father Fiélon. To her speechless look of inquiry he said:

"You are in time, madam, but there is none to lose. We sent for you at the dying man's urgent appeal. Keep a brave heart, and let not your spirit quail at what he may reveal to you."

It was not without trepidation that Carlotta Willoughby entered for the last time into the presence of her cousin, whom she had ever instinctively feared. But he was powerless now to do her harm or to wound her sensitiveness. He was wrestling with the Angel of Death, and his dark, hollow eyes, of unnatural size and brilliancy, appeared to gaze at her from the very threshold of another existence.

"Carlotta," he whispered, feebly, yet with a certain eagerness.

"Cousin Octave, I grieve to find you thus," spoke the

lady, sincerely, for the terrible presence of death banishes all animosities.

"Grieve not for me, sweet cousin, I have been your bitterest foe. But my hate was born of love. You were the desire of my youth, the hope and love of my life. I was not worthy of you; I knew it then—I know it better now. I had thought to carry my secret with me to the grave, not this secret of my love—you know it but too well—but another secret which in this last moment weighs upon my conscience. I cannot receive the last Sacraments nor make my peace with Almighty God until I unburden my soul of its guilt to you."

The dying man here ceased, as if to strengthen himself for what was to come.

"Do not distress yourself, Octave, nor unnecessarily magnify trifling injuries you may have been the cause of," pleaded Carlotta.

"O that they had been but trifling injuries! Alas! Carlotta, I hated Colonel Willoughby. During long years I sought to engage him in a quarrel; he always circumvented me. At last my undying love for you, and my perpetual hate of him, became with me one interwoven, ungovernable passion. I planned his death; I bought his assassins; I remained concealed in ambush, and watched the deadly encounter upon the precipice; I wished to make sure that my enemy was dead. I thought were he out of the way, you might at length be induced to listen to me. More than before, you spurned me from your presence; my guilty conscience told me that you suspected me. Did you suspect me, Carlotta?"

"The thought came to me, but I dared not entertain so horrible a suspicion," replied the lady, ready to faint at this revelation.

"I knew it; therefore, I knew it would be vain to persecute you with solicitations; I formed a plan to capture you, and carry you away from home and children to a distant home, which I had had prepared for you. I was within a few days of carrying out this intention, when your unexpected departure for the North completely baffled me. I then became desperate, and—but my strength fails—ah!"

"Do not further exert yourself," Mrs. Willoughby found strength to utter, but the man continued:

"I have been treacherously slain, even as I caused to be slain your husband. As I have sowed, so have I reaped. But I have made to you, Carlotta, what restitution is possible. I have this morning bequeathed to you legally all I possess, a great portion of which is yours by right of inheritance. It was through my persuasions and false misrepresentations that your father's will was made as it was. It will be all right now for you, but not for me. Do you believe, Carlotta, there is forgiveness in heaven for a wretch like me?"

"Our Lord forgave the thief upon the cross."

"I am more than thief—I am a murderer. The blood of my brother is upon my hands. Do you not see it? Are they not red with blood?" holding up both his hands.

At this moment stepped forward the priest, who had been standing in a far part of the room. He feared the interview would be too exhausting to the lady; besides, he knew it was time for the man to make his last preparation of soul to meet the dread presence approaching.

Carlotta arose to go.

The man placed his hand upon hers detainingly, and said:

"Carlotta, when we were little children you kissed me—once, twice, thrice. I remember the number of times—thrice. Before death seals my lips, kiss me once."

This was said pleadingly, and yet the very soul of Carlotta rebelled. What! kiss the lips of the man or monster who had fiendishly robbed her of her noble husband, slain in his manly prime and beauty! The man who had robbed her and persecuted her, who had made plans for her forced escapade—was not this too much?

All this went through the poor lady's mind, who was ready to faint, and he saw it and shuddered.

"It was a test," he said, sadly. "I thought if you could kiss me, stained as I am, that that would be proof of your forgiveness. If you could forgive me, then I would think God could forgive me; but I blame you not."

In a moment his request was granted; for, like a lightning flash, came to Carlotta's memory the scene upon the cross and the words of the Crucified: "This day shalt thou be with Me in Paradise."

With this kiss of peace was given the last adieu, and the priest taking the lady's place beside the dying man, Carlotta Willoughby withdrew.

Her strength and courage sustained her until she reached her own home, when, bewildered and overcome, she threw herself upon her couch and closed her eyes as if she would fain shut out the memory of what she had seen and heard within the hour.

Before another sunset Octave Geoffrion breathed his last, and on the next to the following day was buried with honors befitting his wealth and influence. For this bad man had his friends. Wealth commands outward respect—and it was not known in Santa Fé, save to the priest and to Mrs. Willoughby, of what crimes he had been guilty.

Thus wealth rightly returned to the widow and children of Colonel Willoughby.

In the early part of another summer came Basil Braun to claim his bride. One year had done much for the youth. He was a man now, with an eye bright and fearless, a brow clear and noble, and a mien dignified and graceful. He found Beatrice like "Barkis, willing." Happily she had become divested of all scruples, and appeared perfectly ready to accept her "vocation" to the dignity and grace of matrimony.

It was a joyous wedding; such another had never been seen at Santa Fé since that of the bride's mother. The great Cathedral was crowded with people at the nine o'clock Nuptial Mass. Dame Maria, a very holy old lady who takes care of the altar and spends a greater part of her time on her knees before the picture of the Virgin and Child, had spared no pains in beautifying every place, picture and appointment. The Most Rev. Archbishop, assisted by several priests, celebrated Mass and performed the ceremony. The black-robed Sisters from both convents came in bodies, followed, the one, by sixty orphans; the other, by a more numerous train of academy pupils. The fine, handsome face of Brother Baldwin, chief of the Christian Brothers, with the first pupils of his new school or college, appeared conspicuously. Francisco was spending his vacation at home, and looked on gravely, seeing his sister given unto another's keeping. Ethel, too, had her place there, but it was among the Sisters; and she wore the white veil which she had taken two days previously. And of all the hearts beating in the grand Cathedral, perhaps none was more content than hers. Quiet and subdued, yet loving and trustful, she again, upon this occasion of the marriage of her friends, offered up the thanksgivings of a grateful heart, that an unseen hand had guided her feet unto a haven of peace.

She has become a fond lover of books, and reads with avidity all that instruct her upon the new religion; and, as she bows her white-crowned brow upon the marriage morn of Basil and Beatrice, her thought of the future is less trembling than that of the bride.

And now that our "Three-Times-Three" is divided, subtracted, and yet remaining, in one sense, entire and a mathematical unity, we pray thee, gentle reader, to join with us in bidding Godspeed to all, and in throwing an old slipper after the bridal twain as they journey downward to their future home in the charming Valley of the Rio Grandé.

www.ingramcontent.com/pod-product-compliance
Lightning Source LLC
Chambersburg PA
CBHW031744230426
43669CB00007B/471